Irresistible Persuasion

The Secret Way To Get to Yes Every Time

Geoff Burch

CAPSTONE
be inspired!
™

This edition first published 2010
© 2010 Geoff Burch

Registered office
Capstone Publishing Ltd. (A Wiley Company), The Atrium, Southern
Gate, Chichester, West Sussex, PO19 8SQ , United Kingdom

For details of our global editorial offices, for customer services and for
information about how to apply for permission to reuse the copyright
material in this book please see our website at www.wiley.com.

The right of the author to be identified as the author of this work has been
asserted in accordance with the Copyright, Designs and Patents Act 1988.

Reprinted December 2010

Library of Congress Cataloguing-in-Publication Data

ISBN 978-1-907-31248-9 (paperback), ISBN 978-0-857-08079-0 (ebk),
ISBN 978-0-857-08098-1 (ebk), ISBN 978-0-857-08099-8 (ebk)

A catalogue record for this book is available from the British Library.

Set in 11.5 on 12.5 Adobe Caslon Pro-Regular by Aptara
Printed in Great Britain by TJ International, Padstow, Cornwall

DEDICATION

To my lovely missus, Sallie. What no one understands is that the computer keyboard is a foreign land to me so I write these books with a crayon and with my tongue lolling. Without my wife's hard work, patience and love, you wouldn't be reading this now.

I would also like to thank my two sons, James and Simon, and their growing families, who never for a moment allow me to get away with being a pompous pillock – thank goodness!

ACKNOWLEDGEMENTS

To: the team at my publishers, Holly, Megan, Iain, and Oriana, who kept me on the straight and narrow throughout the creative process! Thank you.

CONTENTS

CONTENTS

LET'S START AT THE VERY BEGINNING

Businesses fail because they fail to persuade. You may think that this is a sweeping statement but think about it for a moment. The small engineering company collapses because it fails to persuade the bank to lend it any more money. The banks collapse because they fail to persuade the City to make short-term loans against their long-term mortgage lending. The car manufacturer goes under because they cannot persuade the workforce to return to work after a damaging strike – and, perhaps the saddest of all, the new enterprise that never got off the ground because it failed to persuade potential customers to give it a try.

There are so many inspirational and instructive business books that cover everything from management to self belief, but that vital ingredient, persuasion, is never really viewed correctly. Persuasion is a process that, when mastered, can be applied beneficially to all or any aspects of business – or life!

Probably the best way to view this process is as a journey. Imagine for a moment that you are planning a trip. The trouble is that we humans have been travelling for so long that we carry out what is a very complicated procedure in such an automatic way that we don't realize how clever we are being. If we dismantle the process we will see just how sophisticated we have been. Firstly, we decide where we would like to go, and then we make sure we know where we are now. We check out the distance between these two points, decide our mode of travel, the likely obstacles we will encounter, assess the cost and calculate the time required.

You do that every day, from a walk to the shops, a drive to see Aunty Hilda, or a trek around the world. How many times have you failed to reach your destination? Sure, there are unexpected events – we bump into a chum for a chat, there is bad traffic, or we get pursued by ravenous head hunters, but I bet that you have almost never ever failed to get where you wanted to go. In fact, you quite often overestimate the obstacles and come in early and under budget.

For the Aunty Hilda trip, we might employ the aid of a road atlas. Imagine if it was written by a motivational speaker:

"How far is it to Aunty Hilda's town?"

"It's not as far as you think!"

"How do I get there?"

"By believing in yourself!"

"How do I plan the trip?"

"By positively visualizing yourself there!"

A road atlas like that wouldn't remain very long in your possession until it found itself a new career as kindling, yet we tolerate that sort of rubbish in our business lives. When we find ourselves betting our whole future and everything we own on our enterprise, we cannot afford 'ifs and buts'. What is needed is a road map to success – and that is what this book sets out to do.

We must see our pathway to business success in the same way we see a journey. Where do we want to get to? Where are we now? And what obstacles and landmarks do we see along the way? The persuasive skills that we use change as they are applied at different times and to different areas of the enterprise.

Staying with the concept of the journey for a moment, a unique thing about human travel is that we have a fairly clear idea of where we are at any moment in the journey. The early mariners, when out of sight of land, expended a huge amount of effort to try and ascertain where they were at any moment in time. They created instruments such as the sextant and the most accurate timepieces their technology could produce. Why? What does it matter? Leave home, get there, what does it matter what goes on in between?

Well, we know it does matter. Disaster is awaiting the traveller who isn't sure where they are. When planning our trip to Aunty Hilda, we look for all the towns, villages and landmarks along the way and tick them off. If there is one that we weren't looking for, or if we fail to see something we expected, we start to suspect we are going the wrong way – sometimes within minutes of setting off so no real harm done.

So why can't we do it with business?

We start our new business; where are those hordes of new customers, how far away are they from doing business with us? A bit of persuasive marketing will find them. Once we've found them, how do we part them from their cash? Persuasive selling is what you need! As the business soars away, how do you get people to do the work of persuading for you? A bit of persuasive management!

The truth is that you need to stop being you. We tend to buy instructional and motivational books because we are not entirely satisfied with what we are getting. We would like to achieve a change of circumstance without the pain of changing ourselves. The trouble is that the people we envy and admire as being more successful than us have a different attitude, behaviour-set and appearance from us and that is why they get what we don't (yes, I hate them too!). You can imitate them, which works a bit; you could even construct them as a dramatic character and play them as a part, but of course the problem then, as any great thespian will tell you, is that to play a part really well you have to become the person you are playing – which kind of takes us back to square one.

The truth is that the Aston Martin-driving cool guy in the Savile Row suit, Rolex watch and expensive cologne is probably wearing tight rubber underwear, has uncontrolled dreams of strangling guinea pigs, and troubles of his own. This does not take us away from the old but true cliché which states, "If you do what you've always done, you will get what you have always got. If you don't like what you're getting, you will have to change what you are doing."

Can a book change what we do? The one my history teacher whopped me round the head with certainly improved my attention span, and left me with a slight cauliflower ear and an encyclopedic knowledge of the Hundred Years War!

All this book can do is set down the facts and tools that you will need to become more persuasive in everything you do. The problem is you cannot half persuade – your target is either persuaded or not persuaded. Guilty or not guilty. The jury is out on you and your future, and they won't come back with an 'Only a bit guilty' verdict.

Let me reveal a little secret about myself. I take this subject seriously, it's my life's work, it's my career, and it's how I make my money. In other words, I want to be taken seriously but I get criticized for using too many jokes and stories.

John Cleese said, "You don't have to be sombre to be serious." You might notice there will be a waft of psychobabble around this book and it is because I was brought up by a strange Viennese shrink who made me see how the human mind works and how it can be made to work to our advantage. The first example of this is laughter. What is it? The teeth exposed, strange barking and gibbering noises. If you saw a monkey doing this, you would say it was frightened. Maybe jokes touch little nerves of truth that other words don't reach…

So here's the first.

There was this little guy who always felt that he deserved more from life. He was, in his own eyes, a good guy, he prayed regularly not just for himself but for the ills of the world. Yet others, and what he considered to be inferior people, had fate hand them riches. The lottery, for instance, why should the feckless and lazy win millions each week? This time he would pray just for himself.

"Lord, I'm a good guy; let me win the lottery this week."

A week went by with no luck.

"Lord, I've got to say, I'm a bit disappointed with your response. Let me win the lottery, please. I pray regularly, surely I deserve it more than those other dreadful people!"

Another week and still no luck.

"Lord, what is the point in being devout if you let me down like this? Please let me win the lottery!"

Finally, a mighty voice thundered from above.

"Fred! I'm sorry you haven't won the lottery, but meet me half way – BUY A TICKET!"

Who wants you to succeed? Your friends? Maybe, maybe not. We measure ourselves against others and if you, their dear old pal, suddenly start to achieve the things they have failed to, where does that leave them.

Your family? Can they trust you to stay around now you no longer have the failures they can lovingly forgive you for? There are two ways to win a race – either to train hard and be the fastest, or nobble the opposition. Most people will try the second option and win life's race by holding everyone else back.

So who really wants you to succeed? Why me, of course! Just picture the scene in a few years' time. You are on television as one of the five richest people in the world.

"So, to what do you owe your success?"

"Well, I suppose it started when I read this book by Geoff Burch!"

What do you think that this is going to do to my book sales? I'll be up there in the top five with you. Of course I want you to succeed (that, by the way, is a great persuasive lever: 'mutual self interest', 'win-win'), but come half way to meet me, buy a ticket. If we are going to go on this journey together, you must be prepared to do things differently or things won't change for you for the better.

Persuasion is the skill that can transform business, but it needs to be seen as an inevitable journey and over the next pages I will reveal the map.

CHAPTER 1

GET THE MAP OUT

This is where we decide where we are going and we find out where we are now

"Yeah," you said, picking this book up: "I'd like to be able to persuade people to do stuff and buy stuff and give me stuff!"

But what 'stuff'? What exactly do you want from this process? If this was a road map, where precisely do you want to get to?

In that brilliant book, *Alice in Wonderland*, Alice is lost and bewildered. Seeing a weird cat up a tree, she decides to ask it for directions (you have to be a bit bewildered to start asking weird cats directions).

"Excuse me, where do I go from here?"

The Cheshire cat (for it is he ...) replies:

"It all depends on where you want to get to."

Alice says,

"I don't much care where."

The Cheshire Cat rejoins:

"Then it doesn't much matter which way you go, then, does it."

Do You Know Where You are Going?

Look at your map and tell me where exactly on this particular journey you want to get to. Please don't reply with, "Somewhere better than this", or "to get to see the decision maker" or even "more sales".

We need to be a lot clearer in our minds about where we are and where we want to get to if we want to assess how best to get to our destination, the difficulties we are likely to encounter, the time it will take, and the benefits of undertaking the journey in the first place. Vagueness leads to disaster. Retailers have a sort of vague notion that their staff have something to do with the revenue of their business. Ergo, staff could be prevailed upon to help increase the said revenue. Eureka! They need training! Now I do training and, although I say it myself, I feel I'm very good at it.

I have a cat that has the intrinsic intelligence of a tennis ball, but by denying it food I have got it TRAINED to shake hands with me. I will hold out a small piece of cooked meat and this thing will hold out its paw.

"Oh look!" the audience cry, "the kitty is shaking hands with its master."

But, what's the cat thinking?

Is it thinking, "How do you do, master. I'm so sorry that I was unable to join you earlier, but I've just been having a poo in the garden."

Is that what the cat's thinking? I bet its not! The reality is that the cat is thinking nothing at all. Its mind is a complete blank.

The retailer's training regime works on a similar basis. The key is that they train 'how to' not 'why'.

"This is how you greet the customer."

"This is how you present the bag."

"This is how you answer the phone."

But they don't know why they are doing it.

Perhaps you bought this book because you wanted me to show you *how* to persuade. But have you ever considered *why* you should persuade?

Does it matter? Here is a very cruel but funny (so worth doing!) experiment you can try for yourself. Walk into a large high street store, whereupon you will be greeted by a highly trained member of staff.

"Can I help you?"

To which you are supposed to reply, "No thank you, I'm just looking."

For this experiment, change the script and watch the fireworks.

"Can I help you?"

"With what?"

"Pardon?"

"What did you want to help me with?"

"I don't know!"

"Then why did you ask me that?"

Total breakdown! "I don't know why I'm saying it, they make me!"

They literally do not know why they're doing it.

So is it that important to know why things happen or why you are doing what you are doing? I believe that it certainly is – it is an argument I often have with non-mechanical car drivers. When I push the clutch pedal down, I have a picture in my mind of the moving levers and whirling cog wheels. Most people would say, "I press the pedal and the car goes", but when one day that fails to happen and you have no understanding of why it failed to happen, you are left stranded until somebody with understanding comes and saves you. This is exactly the same with the persuasion process; you may learn parrot fashion a number of simple 'how to' phrases, but if you don't understand why you are using them, any failure or deviation from the path you expected could mean disaster. To be a great persuader you have to understand all the cogs and wheels and know why you are doing what you are doing and how that fits into the persuasion journey.

THINK ABOUT THIS

Let's look at our map again. Where do you want to get to on this journey?

This is a great exercise for you to do now!

What is it that you are looking for? Are your answers something like this?

- ✓ I would like a better job.
- ✓ I would like a few big customers.
- ✓ I wish my staff were more loyal.
- ✓ It would be great if each customer spent more.

That is too vague – just pick one.

I would like a few big customers. Like who? Acme Metals Ltd.

- ✓ What have you got to offer them?
- ✓ Who do you need to see there?
- ✓ Who is their current supplier?
- ✓ Why aren't you currently doing business with them if they are such a good target? What on earth have you been doing until now?
- ✓ How far away are they from doing business with you?
- ✓ Is your offer sufficiently robust to keep them as a customer for life?

A Wasted Opportunity

Warning! This book will help you to get opportunities. Don't waste them by going off half cocked. Second chances are very much harder to get (but not impossible – although more of that later).

Read this story and tell me what the guy did wrong (clue, it isn't just one thing, either).

Some time ago I was talking to a room full of business start-ups. Persuasion, I told them, was the skill they needed to get their businesses off the ground. At the back there was a guy who clearly wasn't buying in. Finally he spoke out.

"It's alright for you with your silken tongue and subtle ways. OK, I'm convinced, you could persuade anyone!" (Except him, apparently.) "If I could do what you do I would be up and running. Just give me the chance and watch me go!"

"OK," I said, "Let me help you. I'm yours to command! Who would you like me to persuade on your behalf?"

"Er, um," he looked around the room, and then out of the window he spotted a large office block. He became quite agitated and pointed, "Them!" he cried, "I want an appointment with them. I've got an office cleaning business and that is some office. If I could speak to the decision-maker there, all my dreams would come true!"

"Well," I said, "it just so happens that the CEO of that insurance giant is Sir Jack Thomas, a personal friend of mine. So would you like an appointment with him?"

"Oh yes!"

With this, I picked up the phone.

"Acme Insurance. How can I help you?"

"Oh yes, can I speak to Sir Jack please?"

"Who shall I say is calling?"

"Tell him it's his old pal, Geoff!"

A very fruity voice came on the line. "Geoff! How are you? What can I do for you today?"

"I'm very well indeed, thank you, Sir Jack. I would like a bit of a favour from you please."

"Anything, Geoff, just name it!"

"I've got a chap on one of my courses who has an office cleaning business and he would love an appointment with you."

"Of course, Geoff. Any friend of yours is a friend of mine. When would he like to come?"

"Tomorrow? About 3.00 pm?"

"That would be fine. I'll see him then."

The next day at around 3.00 pm there is a knock at Sir Jack's door.

"Come in!"

Our hero appears with his bag of bits held tight, white knuckled to his chest.

"Oh hello, Sir Jack. It's very kind to you to see me at such short notice."

"No. It's a pleasure. Now tell me all about yourself."

"Well, I was made redundant a few weeks ago and with it being so difficult to get a proper job and that, I decided to start this office cleaning business."

"Oh how enterprising. How is it going?"

"OK, I suppose. I could do with more work."

"Yes, of course. Do you have a leaflet or a brochure?"

"I do. My brother-in-law designed it when he was in prison, during his anger management classes!"

"…and such vivid colours… Well, it has been nice to meet you and can I wish you the very best for the future."

At this, the interview is terminated by a warm smile and firm handshake from Sir Jack. Our hero came galloping back full of excitement.

"What a lovely man. The boss of that huge company. He couldn't have been nicer."

"So have you got the contract to do their office cleaning?"

"Er?"

"Why didn't you ask for his cleaning contract?"

"I didn't want to upset him – he would only have said no."

"Would he?"

"Of course. The place was spotless; he's probably got some-one a hundred times our size doing the cleaning already."

What a waste. I called in a huge favour from someone really influential just so that this half-wit could crouch in their office clutching his bag of assorted grubbiness to his chest for absolutely no reason whatsoever. Perhaps after some counselling we could have more success with the next appointment. What next appointment? Why should Sir Jack ever want to see this idiot again? He had one chance and he blew it.

No Second Chances

I know you haven't read this book yet but at this moment can you see what went wrong?

First, who or what was he going to try and persuade to do what? On our persuasion map that is our destination. Imagine that this book takes away all the hard work, and just by reading it, you will have all the power to persuade anyone to do anything.

The first exercise, setting aside all other things, is who are you going to persuade to do what? Most of us have absolutely no idea. If you are a fan of the self-help gurus, you'll know that they can sometimes drivel on about positive visualization and goal setting.

"Where do you see yourself in five years time?" they say, and then they get you to picture palm-fringed beaches and private jets. In the world of our similarly disingenuous politicians this is macro-thinking; the big picture, life choices. But I am asking you to go back to the simple basic stuff like, "Do you want custard or ice cream?"

Let me ask you again, who do you want to persuade to do what? Until you have answered that, we have no destination on our map and the journey will not start.

What are You Going to Ask for?

Let's go back to our office cleaner and his first of many mistakes. He has started a small office cleaning company that he feels would do well if it had more customers (right!). He saw a large office; they clearly had a large floor area that would need loads of cleaning (right!). This would be a good job for him to have (why does he think that?). What research has he done to discover that this is a customer he should have? (None). He meets the most important man in the company. That man would most likely be very influential in any decisions the company would make (that is right), so what did he ask for from Sir Jack? (Here's a clue, he asked for absolutely nothing.)

So if you were in his place all because your mouth had got you an appointment with someone you weren't ready to do business with, what are you going to ask for?

Just for the moment forget the big picture, the jets, the palms, and the cuddly sunsets. Let's have a look at the small picture. Let me be your Cheshire cat – where do you want to get to?

Our cleaning chum got very agitated when I expounded this thought process to him.

"OK, what would you ask for?" he cried.

During this book I am going to reveal dark secrets, subtleties and techniques but that's for later. Let's jump in with both feet. Forget subtle – it's bull in a china shop time!

"I came here today, Sir Jack, to ask you to give me the cleaning contract for this building, so can I have the cleaning contract please?"

"Ah ha," said my man capering around like a loon, "what if he says no?"

"Well", I said. "What if he says yes?"

"Well, he won't!"

Let's just stop here for a moment. Does our chum – and do you – answer his/our/their own questions? You may as well wake up in the morning, choose all the people you would like to persuade, answer "no" on their behalf and then roll over and go back to sleep.

Can You Read The Queen's Mind?

Some time ago I was training a room full of double glazing salespeople. These people were tough, real foot-in-the-door merchants, whose skill was euphemistically called 'creative selling'. This doesn't mean that they all wore Breton berets, paint-spattered smocks and weren't afraid to cry. What it meant was that when running at full throttle they could 'create' sales out of thin air. Cold-calling was their thing. They could bang on your door and when you appeared partially dressed with a mouthful of still unchewed dinner, could turn your fury into uncontrollable desire for home improvements. They were all getting a bit smug so I said that when in London I had noticed that Buckingham Palace did seem to have a huge number of windows but none of them seemed to be double glazed. I picked out one of these salespeople and asked what the Queen's reaction had been when they had cold-called to set up the appointment.

Try this yourself. Imagine you are this person; what is your reaction? What? You haven't actually asked the Queen? Why not? Stacks of windows to do, plenty of money to pay. Where's the problem? Now you start to list the problems. "I could never get to speak to the Queen." "She wouldn't get involved in stuff like that." "She probably doesn't have a phone number." "I would most likely get locked up in the Tower!" You are predicting trouble and disaster before it happens.

I have to confess that I also wouldn't try and sell double glazing to the Queen, but I feel that I may use a different kind of reasoning which would include a properly-calculated assessment of the profitability of selling to the Royal Family, the accessibility of the Royal Family, and the value that it would bring to me and my business against the enormous investment in time (actually thinking this through, perhaps I should go off and sell double glazing to the Queen; "By Royal Appointment" would look very impressive on my headed notepaper). What I am trying to say is, if you decide against a project through careful evidence-based and reasoned argument, that is not the same as not bothering because you are frightened, prejudiced, or have preconceived ideas. The point is, whoever we are dealing with, whether it is the Queen, the Pope, or Sid next door, unless you are genuinely a mind-reader don't guess the answers to questions you haven't already put to them simply because their status or your timidity has caused you to presume you know what their reply will be.

If You Want to Know What Someone's Answer is Going to be, Ask Them The Question. There is No Other Way.

As you may have guessed, I am not a great fan of cheery "sun'll come up tomorrow" positive thinking and you may find it confusing if you think I'm heading towards the 'BE POSITIVE' frame of mind – which has left me with a really big dilemma. What I am trying to say is, don't be negative. Perhaps cold and calculating would be better – just put away that cheery smile and the tambourine and *THINK THIS THING THROUGH*.

This persuasion thing is a game, a game of strategy, objectives and tactics. Just like chess – up against a Grand Master? "Then he'll wup your arse!" That is a fairly negative prediction of the outcome. Up against a Grand Master? A cheery whistle, a firm handshake and true self-belief will win me every game! The idiot's view. Up against a Grand Master? Maybe he will go for the Molotov-mate, the Perkins Gambit is one of his options. A solid defence and unexpected attack would give me a chance. Knowing this guy's game, he is very strong but does have weakness in the back rank and always castles out of habit. Now that is anticipation.

Prediction is something you do with crystal balls, runes and frogs' entrails. Anticipation is done with knowledge, care, and planning. The essence of this chapter is about knowing where you are going, why you are going there, and how to draw a clearly defined map and plan of how you are going to do it.

POINTS TO PONDER ON CHAPTER 1

1. You cannot plan a journey if you have no idea where you are going.

2. It is very nice to know *how* to do things but not much use if you don't know *why* you are doing them.

3. If your wish-list is too long and too vague, none of your wishes will come true. Remember, even the best genies only give three wishes.

4. Pick a target and make a list of things that stand between you and victory.

5. If hard work or good luck grants you an opportunity, don't waste it; make sure you know precisely how you are going to use this opportunity.

6. Don't answer other peoples' questions in your mind — the only way to get answers is to ask questions face to face.

7. Anticipate, don't predict.

8. Anticipate, don't assume.

CHAPTER 2

THE JOURNEY BEGINS

In which we plan, plot, and equip ourselves for success

Let's start to put our journey together. In the case of our hero, the destination was to win the cleaning contract from Acme Insurance. Let's put that spot on the map. Actually, just hold up there a second – we haven't actually got a map. A few moments ago all we had was a blank sheet of paper with nothing on it at all. Now we have chosen a destination. We have a blank piece of paper with a black spot on it. That is not a map.

Some bright spark suggested that we jot down our life goals on post-it notes and stick them on the wall: to own a Ferrari, to become a film star, or to eat a sticky toffee pudding. That isn't a map either – they are black spots on my blank sheet of life, reminding me of places I'm not. Maps are funny things, our ancient ancestors drew them on parchment, cave walls, and bits of tree bark (the cave wall one didn't survive too well due to its lack of portability) but why the fascination? What makes a map so special?

♩ It shows us where we want to be.

♩ It gives a choice of places we may want to be.

⌄ It shows where we are now.

⌄ It shows how far where we are now is from where we want to be.

⌄ It shows us the obstacles along the way.

⌄ It shows alternative routes that may be longer but avoid the obstacles ('ere be dragons).

A Map of The Real World

The problem for us and our hero is, that if read correctly, maps are also horribly truthful. To return to our post-it note – a Ferrari, to be a film star, or eat sticky toffee pudding – we stick it above our desk and when we glance up it gives us hope. When the instruction came from my publisher to write a book on persuasion, I was not asked to write a book on hope. If we take the average Joe and, as an outsider, we assess how realistic his post-it notes are, we may judge:

⌄ The Ferrari – not a hope

⌄ Film star – not a hope

⌄ Sticky toffee pudding – easy (but will make him fatter and even less likely to be a film star)

But if we now apply the map thing, we should achieve a different result – possibly even some kind of inevitability. The thing with maps is they are not simply a statement of destination or even a list of destinations. What they actually do is give us a number of destinations to choose from, and by looking at the map we can see where we are now, our current position and we can choose a destination and see the obstacles in between. When we see this clearly in black and white we can plan our journey – or if the obstacles are too daunting we could abandon the trip altogether and choose an easier destination. But without an accurate map none of these things are possible.

The Ferrari Map

Question: Where am I now?

Answer: I currently don't own a car and have no driving licence. I do own my own house and the mortgage is half paid.

Now we can put that second point on the blank sheet – the one that states current position.

The truth is that if this guy sells his house he could have a Ferrari – job done.

"But," he wails, "where would I live?"

"Oh, so you want a house *and* a Ferrari but at the moment the house is more important than the Ferrari?"

Perhaps he doesn't want a Ferrari at all. What he maybe wants is the status and standard of living that people who own Ferraris usually have. There is more to this, but for now let's learn to be more precise about our destination.

Worse Things Happen at Sea

It's all well and good having the map, but you should also know where you are on the map at all times. I have a small sailing boat which, due to my closet desire to be a pirate and lack of ability, tends to be the bane of all who know me. Shipwrecks are a fairly regular occurrence, much to the terror of my long-suffering crew (usually my traumatized missus). One of the key features of a good shipwreck is hitting things that you should have known were there. To find out where the things not to hit are, you use a map – or to pacify the yachties, the correct name is a chart ('ere be sea monsters). To the uninitiated, looking at a nautical chart tells you sod all – after all, it's a map of water sometimes with bits of land on it which are one of the things to avoid hitting, but mostly it's a map of water. You would think a map of water would be a fairly blank page but these charts are full of symbols, numbers, little arrows, pictures of compasses and indications of things under the water – which are other things not to hit. I was finally sent by my mutinous crew to night school to learn how to read these charts. Let me tell you they are very, very difficult to use. If you failed trigonometry, astronomy, maths and geometry as I did, you are sunk (literally).

These charts are also very very expensive, yet before you set off on a voyage you write all over them (admittedly with pencils), planning your trip. Then as you bob along, you set down where you really are – they call it plotting (which is great because we are going to do lots of plotting later), which is often not where you thought you were going to be. This comes as no surprise to the salty sea dog who makes course corrections to allow for tidal drift and wind. The trick is to know where you are at any given moment – not easy because it involves triangulation from landmarks, leading lights, shooting compasses and unrecognizable planets or stars. Then one day, eureka! A magic box of techno tricks called a GPS appears. Satellite navigation – a little plastic box that tells you exactly where you are at any moment. You don't have to know where you are, you just tell it where you would like to be and it guides you there. Burn the charts, bin the dividers and snap the pencils.

But what happens when you get in to trouble? As you sink beneath the waves, it may be time to radio the lifeboat.

"'Ello sir, where exactly are you sinking?"

As the saltwater creates a jolly little firework display of blue sparks from the boat's electrics and the GPS screen goes blank, you realize that you have absolutely no idea whatsoever.

"Have a look at your chart and tell us where you were when you last marked it. Within the last half hour will do!"

"Um…"

"OK then, where have you come from?"

"I know where I want to get to."

"Well, you won't be doin' that now sir, will you."

"What shall I do?"

"Send up a flare and hope that our helicopter can see it. If not, we'll inform your nearest and dearest!"

The point is, if you are a yachtie, however advanced technology becomes, you still need to be able to use and read a paper map. The same lesson applies to us – it is just so easy to Google a name or a company and call it 'desk research' when in reality what we really need is a good thick pad of paper, a stubby pencil, and the burning of plenty of midnight oil. If we depend on our Blackberry, Google, or any other technological wizardry, we will never have a firm grasp in black and white writing of our planned route between our starting point and our chosen destination. Particularly on the route to persuasion we can expect a lot of unexpected deviations along the way which our written chart can show us.

The lesson is, it's not just about the destination, it's about the seen and unseen obstacles along the way. We should never lose sight of where we come from and where we currently are in relation to where we want to get to. We should have a clear, and preferably written, note of exactly where we are and how that relates to where we are planning to be. Otherwise we may find ourselves cast adrift if the journey doesn't go exactly according to plan.

We should also be guided by our own senses and investigation of where we are, not some computer or a person telling us how great we are or how well we are doing. If you can't measure the distances covered accurately, it is virtually impossible to understand the challenges of the journey or to clearly access where you are. Careful measurement is the essence of the successful journey – in other words, you always need to know where you are even if that knowledge is a little bit depressing.

Are You Qualified?

We need to introduce a very powerful word into our persuasion vocabulary and that is 'qualify'. It seriously affects both the 'persuader' and the 'persuaded'. Every sales training or persuasion book obsesses about qualifying the subject, the 'persuaded', which we cover throughout the rest of this book, but it is important to firstly check on our own qualifications to satisfy the promises that we make to our subjects. A cheesy old cliché which is apposite in this case is, watch out when you point a finger at someone because three fingers are pointing back at you. It always makes me smile when I see the scruffy, ill-groomed car salesman, reeking of tobacco and cheap aftershave, talking about the customer as being a 'tyre kicker' and not being qualified to purchase a car from him. I think as a customer I would ask myself whether he was qualified to sell to me. So, let's first look at the persuader. They need to convince people to give them a chance to become, say, a film star, as on the post-it list above.

Let's list their features – a bit plain-looking (I was going to say stunningly ugly but that can give unique appeal, just think of Charles Laughton or Margaret Rutherford), a bit shy, and absolutely no acting ability whatsoever (even that doesn't seem to have held back our current crop of child actors so I suppose there's hope). I am completely tone deaf and have no sense of rhythm so if I put on my motivational post-it note 'Lead violinist with the Vienna Symphonia' there simply cannot be any map to draw and there is no route from where I am (tone deaf) to where I want to be (lead violin). In other words I am not, and will not ever, be qualified.

As a positive thinking book we fail a bit here because, apparently, positive visualization can bring anything, but in this case we don't have positive visualization. We have ice cold calculated planning, and if our destination is genuinely not attainable we have actually saved ourselves a lot of time and heartbreak trying to reach it. In this happy clappy world where none can fail and cynicism (I call it realism actually) is the biggest crime you can commit, we watch with horror when kids, asked about their future, state "I am going to be famous!"

"For what?" you howl.

For you, this is good. It is the first step to understanding the power of qualification. "For what?" is the question we must ask of ourselves. OK, a film star with no talent is not quite as tricky as a violinist with no talent, so it's possible, but when drawn as a map the huge difference between current position and destination may make the less tenacious, or more realistic traveller, abandon the project for something easier. There is little point in lusting after a visit to the North Pole if you lack the funds, the fitness, the equipment, or the tenacity to get there. If any one of these elements is missing it might be better to accept failure in the initial planning stage and do something about it rather than be found some years later frozen to an iceberg. The planning and the map will literally tell us if we are qualified to undertake the journey.

Here is another health warning. In a previous book I have likened the ability to persuade to a martial art, one that can be learned and mastered but, like all martial arts, if not used responsibly and intelligently can have very difficult consequences.

For me, the power to persuade was a sort of reflex thing that I developed as a kid. We all do it – some of us get rid of the bully by making him laugh, others become studious to get the approval and protection of the teachers, some become stronger and fitter and give the bully a hiding. I found I could persuade the bully to go and hit someone else. As I got more skilful, a sort of weird laziness set in as I discovered that everything in the world that you could ever want is in the gift of someone else (from food to political office). If they can be persuaded there is nothing you cannot have, but – and it is a huge but – if you are not qualified, some of the things you get you may wish you hadn't.

I watched a wildlife programme recently where a large but stupid predatory fish had died trying to swallow an opponent of similar size. This is a clear example of literally biting off more than you can chew. If your skill as a persuader takes you beyond your ability as a deliverer you can cause yourself an enormous amount of heartache, so be careful!

So ask yourself at the start whether you are qualified and equipped to complete this journey.

A very sad little story here. A lot of very, very beautiful film stars found it extremely difficult to find love, particularly Marilyn Monroe. Men heard that she wanted a normal ordinary partner, and normal ordinary men queued up, but none of them lasted very long with her lifestyle. Seemingly unrelated, but bear with me, a mass market car maker dictated that the dealers put its mid-range family saloons in the window, but one dealer also had, bizarrely, the Ferrari franchise and insisted on putting a fiery red Ferrari in the window. He was regularly berated for doing this but he continued. The manufacturer was going to punish him, until it discovered that he sold about twice as many boring family saloons as everyone else. Why? It's the beautiful film star thing – a day with Marilyn or a test drive in a Ferrari. But come on, guys, are you qualified to own one? As you sit in the six-screen multiplex cinema munching your popcorn, are you really enjoying the film or are you wondering what the feral kids are doing to your Ferrari in the car park. When you pull up at the lights and the guy in the car next to you with a little lip curl wishes a bit of bankruptcy on you to cut you down a peg or two – can you take that? When your gorgeous starlet wife is in a screen embrace with George Clooney or Antonio Banderas, is she comparing them to you? The men came in to run their hands over the Ferrari but were prepared to leave with the family saloon.

Actually what happened was that the big manufacturers spotted this in the sixties and created the Mustang, the Capri, the Charger, and the Camero, family saloons that looked sporty, went like the clappers, would get you safely to work every day, and could take the family on holiday.

The moral here is that when qualifying your subject, of course don't under-shoot, but also don't over-shoot your target either.

Get The Right Equipment

Before starting out, as for all big adventures, we need to be correctly equipped. If it's the North Pole we want, it's no good packing just a Hawaiian shirt and flip-flops. Our proto film star should learn to act, take confidence classes and start work on their appearance. More relevant to us, is our office cleaning chum capable of taking on and sustaining such a big contract? We should always treat every persuasion project like an expedition, and in the planning stage we should take a pad of paper and a pen and set down in writing the equipment – both physical and mental – that we will need to take with us to achieve a successful outcome.

It doesn't do any harm to write down your wish list and then, just like a polar expedition, set down your equipment needs. Mostly our equipment is mental in the persuasion process – do we have a clear understanding of where we want to get to? Have we anticipated all the possible objections or concerns of the subject? In a more physical sense, do we have written proof and evidence of what we are claiming, i.e. testimonials, brochures, price lists, presentations? Perhaps optimistically, if romance was our game, do we have a stout knee protector and a diamond ring in our pocket! It is no good seeing the moon rise gently above the azure sea, as the lapping wavelets attune to the distant sounds of a Hawaiian guitar, to then discover you have forgotten the ring. More seriously, every great explorer not only makes sure they have plenty of the correct equipment, but they ensure that it is clean, serviceable, and up to date. The number of times I have met someone who has attempted to persuade me with a bulging briefcase full of dog-eared, out-of-date brochures, irrelevant paperwork, and corrected price lists. You know who you are going to see, you have reasonably defined parameters of what you are trying to persuade them to do, so why are you carting about piles of irrelevant rubbish? Before each meeting, start with a completely empty portfolio and select from your immaculate files the clean, precise, and up-to-date pieces you will need for this specific project.

 A WARNING

Please enjoy the power this book will give you but, like all power, use it responsibly and when you persuade others to give you a chance, make sure you are qualified to fulfill your promise.

To Win The Acme Insurance Cleaning Contract What Should We Ask?

- ✓ Do we have the skill sets for this customer's special needs?
- ✓ What proof do I have that we have these skills?
- ✓ Can we meet all of this customer's demands without slip-up?
- ✓ Will we surprise and delight this customer with a level of service that exceeds his expectations?
- ✓ As the boss of my company, when I meet this client do I give the impression that I am more – or at least as – professional as anyone else he would meet in the course of his professional career?
- ✓ Does my company's literature, vehicles, and team behaviour reflect in every way that kind of professionalism?

If you are thinking, "Here, hang on a minute, this isn't persuasion, I would willingly give my business to a company like that, I don't need persuading", that *is* persuasion. It isn't just subtle words, it is how you look and what you do.

POINTS TO PONDER ON CHAPTER 2

1. Just writing down a wish or desire is not planning. You can't have a map without a start, a finish, and a bit in-between.

2. If we write down our desires, we also need to write down where we are now. It might be a bit depressing but it brings a bit of realism into the game.

3. If we plan our persuasion campaign like a sailor planning a voyage, we can predict the obstacles and delays and we should know where we are at any given moment.

4. Be sure, when you set a goal, that it is the goal that you really want and not just the one you imagine it to be.

5. On any expedition, we have to make sure that we have the correct and appropriate equipment.

6. Be careful what you wish for, you might get it.

7. Make sure you are qualified to handle the rigours of the journey.

PART TWO

THE JOURNEY

CHAPTER 3

MONEY GROWS ON TREES

In which we discover the power of belief and desire against the fear of risk

Here is a fascinating head game that can give you some great insight into persuading others. Sometimes we have to give a bit to get a bit, but it can be a mistake to give too much. For this exercise we have to assume that you would like to be a millionaire.

Guess what! It's your lucky day. A person, casually dressed (actually a bit trampy-looking), arrives at your door with a small shrub in a pot. They explain that this unlikely looking plant is a money tree that is about to flower at any moment and produce a crop of millions of large denomination bank notes. They are prepared to let you have it for fifty pounds cash.

Please play the game here, I promise it will give you fabulous insights. What is the first question you ask him if you haven't already slammed the door?

I bet it's, "Why don't you use it?"

The reply is, "Well, I have and I'm fabulously wealthy but being a magical tree it only grants its owner one crop. So now it's your turn!"

Well go on, do it! Give him the cash and your money worries will be over. I actually sell these trees myself and if you send me the cash I will send you your money tree by return. What is stopping you? What is the thought process that is going on in your head right now?

Is it that you don't want the money? No?

Is it that you think that £50 is too much to pay to be a millionaire? No?

So what is it? It is a lack of belief. It is a lack of trust. Magic trees in your previous experience have been a bit of a letdown. The character on your doorstep doesn't look that rich or believable.

Too Good to be True?

Apply these tests now to your offering. Perhaps you could save your client money, be better in every way than their current supplier. Perhaps you could bring them eternal happiness – yet they bin your mailers, they won't give you appointments and, if they do, you get nowhere near getting the business. A bit of harsh honesty here: are you a bit like the guy with the money tree? Clearly your potential client should want the benefits you offer, yet they simply don't appear to trust you to deliver them. They don't believe what you say.

Trust Me!

You walk up to someone and say, "Buy my home improvement, it will pay back its cost in savings in just six months and go on for another twenty five years to save you thousands! How about it?"

Are you seriously telling me they don't want to save thousands? No! They don't believe what you are saying. They are saying you are untruthful.

They are in essence calling you a liar.

Before you get too upset about that, isn't that just what you felt about the money tree man? What has he got to do to convince us? Maybe he should look the part – if he arrived in a helicopter wearing a Saville Row suit it might help, but you could smell a bit of a conman rat.

I was telling this story to a group of people and someone said that she would believe in him if he was an eight-foot-tall demon who had exploded through a fiery hole in the floor in a sulphurous cloud of smoke! If you read the story of Faustus, the man who sold his soul to the devil to fulfill certain wishes (there was loads of highfaluting stuff but I think there was a pretty woman involved somewhere, silly old fool!), you will notice that the devil had to appear in a selection of guises before Faustus was convinced that he was dealing with the decision maker, as it were.

It's Magic

If you sell a magic product, be magical in everything you do. Many years ago there was a TV series called 'The Avengers' which stood aside from the other telly shoot-em-up programmes because the characters were so surreal. If the action took place around a flower shop, the man would be called Mr Bloom and his team would all be festooned in flowers. If they were the hit men (which they often were), their victim would be found in a bed of roses. It is congruent with the offer and the whole atmosphere supports the promise. Look around you – that nasty aggressively driven van says 'Trustworthy Professional Service' on the side! Does that gibbon at the wheel look trustworthy or professional? Worse, does he work for you? See the restaurant with 'Best food in town' written in the window along with the dead flies and dog pee stain by the door.

You have got to get your offer right.

Why do I need to tell you this? Most of us know how to do it, it's just that we fail to recognize the importance to our current persuasion project or, worse, we can't be bothered.

Lucky in Love

Do another mental exercise for me. Just imagine you are single and your destination in this plan is a partner in love. Do a little bit of research into where to find your likely prospects.

Now here's a thought. We are already conjuring up partners in our mind that we are 'qualified' to persuade. Think back to 'Are You Qualified' in the previous chapter. If we have a modest income, the polo field may be a tough area to be impressive in. If we are over 50, the techno all-night rave might be a little out of our league.

So we are identifying the most likely targets and the areas in which we will find them. If you have got teenage kids, you will know that it is almost impossible to get them clean or cooperative, but just watch them when romance is in the offing; the hair products, perfumes, colognes, the very best clothes, and sometimes even washing. They are instinctively trying to become qualified. They are absolutely clear about what they want and they know that any slip-up in the dress, coolness or smelliness department dramatically reduces their chances.

We all used to be able to do that, so why do we now arrive at a business meeting/job interview/sales pitch thinking, "These shoes are a bit scuffed but oh well", or are we hot and smelly from rushing? Or do we have a bag full of the wrong literature or price lists that have been corrected with biro? Perhaps our shop could do with a lick of paint; the windows don't get cleaned as often as they should. Why pay a professional designer or sign writer when bonkers cousin Terry is a bit of a dab hand with a paint brush? Do you think that will seduce the customers? No, nor do I!

Don't Make It Hard on Yourself

This book should give you the power to persuade and yes, I believe anybody can be persuaded to do anything. With enough energy the sceptical and even antagonistic can be brought around to your point of view, but why make things difficult for yourself. Yes, you could, I suppose, get to the North Pole in flip-flops and a Hawaiian shirt but I don't fancy it.

Imagine that you are always going out for romance. Is everything about you, your offer, your premises, your people and your vehicles, ready to persuade? When people see you, do they judge that you are qualified to provide what they want?

If you want to test this for yourself, put yourself in the mind of a customer and walk the high street shop by shop as I did while researching my television show for the BBC, *All Over the Shop*. Who would you do business with and why? Who wouldn't you do business with and why? The cafés and restaurants – would you eat there or not? Flick through the *Yellow Pages* and look at the trade advertisements. Who is attractive and who is not? Look at vehicles – could the owners tarmac your drive or would you call the police?

Then go back again and imagine you had been given those businesses to put right. What would you do? Can you see why you weren't attracted? Now, as a stranger, look back at your own offering and make these changes.

The Risk Factor

To sum up this whole exercise, we now need to understand a bit about the psychology of what's going on. It is all about risk. As human beings we have an in-built and instinctive desire to avoid risk. It is part of our genetic programming that has kept us safe for thousands of years.

You didn't buy the money tree because you felt that you risked losing fifty pounds. Hey, let's give you the money tree business. How would you change the structure and offer of Money Tree Inc to reduce that feeling of risk in our potential customers? First, appearance; looking rich might be persuasive, but looking magical would be better.

An Offer You Can't Refuse

Let me put another offer to you. I appear on your doorstep with said shrub, still a bit scruffy, but with a different offer.

"I know this sounds crazy, but can I ask you, would you like one hundred thousand pounds?"

What is your reply? Sceptical? Disbelieving? Maybe, but surely you would like a hundred thousand pounds.

"Go on."

"I would like to give you this tree as a gift – no cost, purely a present to you. The only thing is that this thing is a money tree that can no longer function for me, but within 24 hours of your ownership it should produce a crop of around a million pounds. If you return 900,000 pounds to me, it will leave you 100,000 pounds for your trouble!"

"What if there is no crop of money?"

"Then you haven't lost anything. I am offering you one hundred thousand pounds and a free shrub for just for a few moments of your time."

Look back at the original offer, a straight fifty quid buy, or the current one. Which one will you choose? It is amazing how many people go for the second. Why? Because it is risk free.

Do you realize that to avoid the risk on this deal you are prepared to pay EIGHTEEN THOUSAND TIMES MORE!

How Can This Story Help Us?

↲ People want loads of benefits but they also fear risk. Therefore people want maximum benefit at minimum risk. When we set out to persuade, we pile on the benefits without considering the other person's concept of risk. "Book us for your daughter's wedding and we will chuck in the cars, the champagne and the band!" "I have one daughter, one wedding on one day. If you cock it up, it will be a true disaster!" Actually it would be great if customers would really speak their thoughts like that because then we could do something about it (that is why later on we are going to learn a bit of benign interrogation).

J The reduction of risk is why we use third party recommendations. If the guy next door has used the money tree and it has worked for him, get him to tell his neighbour.

J For some bizarre reason, machinery salespeople have this uncontrollable desire to demonstrate their product – in fact they go off on courses to learn how to do it. They call it the 'dem' and they insist on doing one on you or to you (I'm not sure of the correct 'dem' grammar) but they have no idea why they are doing it. They should be doing it to prove that whatever it is can do the required job and can be purchased without risk. If I could demonstrate the money tree then you would buy it.

J Of course manufacturers have been doing it for years: 'Free Home Trial', 'Money back guarantee', 'If you aren't delighted, we will return double the amount you paid', 'Send no money'. Maybe they don't know why they are doing it but they know it works. It works because it reduces risk.

J If you can get down to the 'what the hell…' money, if the tree was a fiver with some of the money going to a kids' charity, you would buy it with a 'what the hell…' attitude. We love to get just a little bit ripped off. We can enjoy the risk without the danger. We go to the carnival with our kids and at the rifle booth we pay a couple of pounds for a go. Then we whisper that carnival folk are people of the night, brigands, waiting to dupe the unwary. The gun sights are twisted so the shrewd riflemen look along the barrel instead. And sure enough, to the chagrin of the stall holder, the five tin soldiers fall, winning you a small weird furry thing that costs the stall holder 50p – thereby giving him 400% profit and you a feeling of outwitting the unwittable. You're both happy so what the hell!

J Understand how much people give to avoid risk. Home trials, money back guarantees – give them that, sure, but understand the value of them. If you give those reassurances you don't need to cut prices.

POINTS TO PONDER ON CHAPTER 3

1. People always want benefits but will do anything to avoid risk.

2. Look the part! If you don't, it increases the sense of risk in the other person.

3. Sometimes our subjects will express a desire for something that exposes them to too much risk and will actually go for the safer option.

4. Be aware that all our tools, brochures, cards, and demonstrations, if professionally presented, all help to allay that feeling of risk. If done badly, it increases it.

CHAPTER 4

I DIDN'T EXPECT THAT

In which we show how the power of
persuasion can control the future

A few thoughts about marketing, job offers, and selling.
They all have one thing in common and that is they
start the persuasion process with the creation of an expectation. If you are the person to be persuaded, before this
happens you must have in you a feeling of expectation
and it must be an expectation of an improvement in your
current circumstances, or at least prevention of a worsening
in current circumstances. We have in us a genetic disposi-
tion to constantly improve our position. Maybe this is what
sets us aside from all other living creatures that simply want
to survive and reproduce. It is rare that we are filled with
tranquil contentment at our current situation and, if we are,
we see it as a sort of break or holiday that sets us up for our
next upward climb.

**Therefore, to persuade we need to hold out the hope
of an improvement in circumstance or the prevention of
a decline.**

In a fire

Follow me, I can see the exit!

In a robbery

Give me your money and I won't shoot you.
In an advert
Use Sniffo and become attractive (actually it would probably say 'more attractive', thereby stating that your current
situation, although attractive, could actually still be improved
to more attractive).
In love
Darling, be mine and I will waft you away to a place of
pure ecstasy!

Things Can Only Get Better

As I write this, I have a thought that I find hard to challenge and it is this: I don't think that it is possible to
persuade without the offer, promise, or perception of an
improvement in the current circumstances, or protection
from trouble. Therefore we must understand the current
circumstances, the person we are persuading must understand their current circumstances, they must develop or be
shown dissatisfaction with their current circumstances – or
the threat of dissatisfaction with it in the future – and we
must demonstrate a believable ability to improve that situation, or to help them to avoid losing what they have and of
staying safe.

I Can See The Future

It is all about things that are going to happen in the future.
Again, as a species, what sets us aside from other creatures
is our ability to use intellect to predict the future. It is both
a blessing and a curse. In the Garden of Eden, the terrible
fruit that brought the ruin of mankind came from the Tree
of Knowledge or perhaps fore-knowledge. For Darwinians
it still works: imagine the happy monkeys gibbering around
in trees until they became old and fell dead on to the forest
floor below – still with a cheery grin that had been with
them all their lives. Then one day, as evolution had slowly
done its work, the first monkey had developed a bit of

language and some ability for abstract thought. It, seeing its stricken colleague plummet through the trees and bounce on to the ground, thought to itself, "Oh no. That's going to happen to me one day."

And so, on that great day in the history of mankind, we moved from monkey to the first paranoid neurotic!

It is pointless using persuasion on animals because they cannot visualize a future event. Maybe the proffered titbit can offer a very short-term concept of instant gratification, but really with animals it is conditioning not persuasion. (By the way, the animal bit of humans and the use of human conditioning gives us some very powerful tools but we will look at that in the psychology bit.)

I always feel very uneasy about eating animals because I tend to anthropomorphize them and the more human they look the less likely I am to eat them. It is hard to explain to the less sensitive that I will eat chicken and fish; I tried to explain this to my butcher by saying I won't eat anything with a face on it. As a bluff country lad, his reply was, "Nothing has a face on it when I've finished."

A Happy Pig is a Dead Pig

That isn't quite what I meant. Some Spanish friends keep a pig which is a sort of pet. The children play with it and give it fruit from the orchard where it snuffles about amongst the roots contentedly doing piggy things. All things considered, a very happy piggy indeed. Then on a special day, with a band, banners, and lots of wine, the whole village appears to decorate and pet the pig. The pig is so joyful to be the centre of attention and it grunts little grunts of piggy joy. The owner creeps up behind it and gives it a massive whack on the head. Its throat is slit and traditionally the children play with the blood which is made into a special sausage which has to be eaten on this pig-festival day. The rest of the animal is jointed up, shared and turned into ham. I was horrified. "How cruel!" My Spanish friend said, "You are the ones who are cruel. You people keep your pigs locked away from the light, from love, from the fresh air, and before they are even mature enough to know the world you put them in trucks and drive them miles in terror to die in a death factory where they can hear the squealing of the other dying pigs. Our pig was a happy pig that had the best of piggy lives. Death was not expected and when it died, it died happy in its own home."

I had made the mistake of not realizing that pigs have no concept of future. It was happy to be happy (I still didn't eat any of it though!).

Jam Tomorrow

We do have a concept of the future, and it is the promise of a better future that gives us the power to persuade.

In the persuasion business we have a problem right from the start. If we go back to the money tree in the previous chapter for a moment, we have to consider that first contact – the first impression.

The conflict that we have is that the person we are trying to persuade has to become excited about some future event, namely the huge crop of money that they will harvest. Again we come up against the fact that the event we are trying to persuade about takes place in the future. It hasn't happened; there is no evidence of something that hasn't happened yet. You could say that time travel could take you to the past and make things happen yesterday, but as you haven't done that yet, even time travel can only happen in the future.

Most of you reading this are probably very sceptical about magic and time travel. The money tree fails to convince you for a number of reasons.

- ᒐ You have had no direct personal experience of a magic product that has functioned. It would be different if you lived in Oz or Middle Earth, therefore let's consider the environment we create for our pitch.
- ᒐ You know of no one you trust who has experience of functioning magical products.

◡ The person selling the money tree is not congruent with the whole magic thing.

◡ The person's demeanour and appearance raise mistrust.

◡ The money tree is not currently carrying a crop of money. This is key because we have to be convinced that this will happen in the future.

◡ The deal, in our perception, is too good to be true.

◡ This is the very first we have heard of this person and the money tree. If they had been on television chat shows, if there were dozens of glossy adverts in the prestige magazines and on TV, or if the person was a recognizable celebrity, we may be more open to listen.

If it was someone we know very well who has in the past been trustworthy in other areas, we may also be more receptive.

The Conman's Handbook

I realize that, set down, these ideas may seem blindingly obvious but it is very rare that we consider the other person's situation in these terms. My wife threw a wobbly when I suggested that the title of this book could be *The Conman's Handbook*, but I was probably only half joking. There is a lot to be learned from con artists, and if we go over those rules again we can see that the classic con understands and deals with most of them.

The con artist is very careful to create exactly the correct impression, whether it is as a beautifully dressed, manicured and perfumed international success, or as a bit of an idiot who is too daft to see that the tatty old print they have to sell for a few hundred is clearly a genuine Leonardo da Vinci cartoon (fat chance!).

They are scrupulous about the environment they choose. If they are going to sell you Big Ben, they will probably meet you in 10 Downing Street and then seal the deal with supper at the House of Lords. They will give you previous experience by letting you win. The first little fifty pound money tree will have a crop of a few thousand, the next day the thousand pound money tree doubles that. Why mess about? Re-mortgage the house and go for the five hundred thousand pound tree and scoop the pot.

Can you see that because we naturally distrust the future, the skilful operator has to sell themselves first?

The Devil Knows Best

When criticized for his rousing music, William Booth of the Salvation Army said, "I don't see why the devil should have all the best tunes." It is the same for me. I meet people whose businesses and even lives could be improved by them being a bit more convincing, but when the discussion starts there is all sorts of nervous squirming about being 'pushy', 'blowing my own trumpet' or 'high pressure selling'.

Look, if you are reading this book, if you want more business, better prices, a good job, or even more luck in love, the chances are that you are a good honest person who deserves some lucky breaks and you will give great satisfaction when the time comes to deliver, yet the con artists of this world are running rings around you. They convince the people you should be convincing and then they deliver nothing. All I am saying is don't let the devil have the best techniques.

Our first step, then, on this journey on the road to persuasion is to convince the other party that they can expect a better, more secure future. Think about what you offer and apply that thought. Here are some examples:

A coffee bar – come in, rest your feet, relax, and enjoy a great coffee that will set you up for the day.

Insurance company – if anything should happen, we can save you from loss and protect you.

The Mafia – we can protect you.

A manufacturer – we can save you money.

When you meet your prospect, what golden future are you going to offer them?

We have a huge danger building for us right now, because if our livelihood depends on our ability to convince, the temptation is to promise anything just to get that chance. Can I even suggest that at times we are even a little dishonest? Wot, you? Really?

One of my favourite business thinkers is a guy called Ricardo Semler who runs one of Brazil's largest corporations in a most astonishing way. (I recommend his books – they will amaze and fascinate you.) I had the chance to meet him and he was going on in the most entertaining way about how useless conventional staff recruitment was. He said it was like internet dating. Imagine internet dating – if you haven't had any experience of it. Describe yourself on the web page. Pick a photo from your album, tell us your age. Is that really you? Come on, be honest, was that picture taken a few years ago when you were a few pounds lighter?

Now what do you think your prospective partner is doing? Yep! Exactly the same.

"I look a lot like Angelina Jolie!"

"What a coincidence. I'm the spitting image of Daniel Craig!"

I think someone is going to get a surprise. Don't you feel just a bit uneasy when you create your CV? Why you left your last job, your ambitions, your crushing desire to be a team player, but before you feel too guilty or start to beat yourself up about it, bear in mind that your prospective employer is up to exactly the same tricks. Consider your last period of employment. Were you blissfully happy, did you relish every moment that you were at work? What did the job advertisement say? Pick up a paper, turn to the recruitment pages and read any job ad:

Can you work with people?
Would you like a more tranquil, slower pace of life?
You will drive a luxury car, usually a Rolls Royce.
Great benefits await the right applicant at…Heavenly Dispatch. We are God's Travel Agent.

An undertakers. After all, they never said the people you worked with would actually be alive. Disappointment all round.

Ricardo solved this quite simply by saying to job applicants, "Come in and work with us for a few weeks, try a few different jobs. If you love it, tell us what you expect to be paid. If we love you, we can offer you a more permanent job but you won't know until you've tried." (By the way, that is a hugely powerful classic selling technique called the Puppy Dog Close, but that is for later!)

Promises, Promises

In the sales process, particularly in large companies, sales become detached from the business in hand and, dare I say it, the real world. They are given a very simple objective and that is, "Sell More!" We will go through the selling process in some detail later, but for now the easiest way to increase sales is to make great promises for the future. Truth be told, some salespeople feel that they can promise anything to win the order but even those of us who are scrupulously honest get tempted when under pressure.

"Well, come on! If you want this order today I must be reassured you will definitely deliver no later than a week on Friday. Well?"

You know that's a bit iffy but you could walk out with a big fat order.

Can you see a pattern yet?

We create our first big step on the pathway to persuasion by **creating expectation**:

⌣ Expectation – of a job well done.

⌣ Expectation – of a problem solved.

⌣ Expectation – of a dream fulfilled.

Marketing is where the art of creating expectation is at its highest. It is also where most small businesses fail.

Jam Tomorrow – or Trouble Tomorrow?

This is a book on persuasion, not on morality or conflict resolution. Our skill as a persuader can present us with some very stark choices. The marketers and customer care gurus say we should always under-promise and over-deliver, whereas the public would probably accuse most salespeople of doing exactly the opposite – in other words over-promising and under-delivering. The problem is, if you under-promise too much you won't get the chance to deliver anything. They say that the meek shall inherit the earth – that is only as long as no one else wants it. So our choice is this: to be more self-effacing and diffident about our promises, and accept we will get less chances but every one of our subjects will be surprised and delighted; or we can over-promise, create expectations that we suspect we can't fulfil which will provide us with a lot more opportunities, but also with a lot more arguments and angry lynch mobs. If I was giving advice, I would say we have to pick a very fine balance between these two extremes and the main point is, once armed with these powerful persuasion tools, you must go into every interaction with your eyes open, and know how much you can deliver and how well prepared you are for trouble if you can't. The whole essence of this book is controlled persuasion which is about meticulous planning and knowing where you are at every stage and this is just as vital in the area of managing expectations as anywhere else in the persuasion process.

POINTS TO PONDER ON CHAPTER 4

1. Everything we offer will happen in the future.

2. Only humans can anticipate and therefore fear the future. When we persuade, all we can do is create an expectation of the future. People may resist our persuasion because they have fear of what will happen in the future.

3. We must build trust before anyone can accept what we have planned for their future.

4. If we can offer samples, we should make them wonderful as they are a taste of the future we are offering.

5. We must understand that our promises should either hold out a promise of continued safety or future improvement.

6. Conmen can con because they are believable. You could fail because you are not, even if you are offering the most value and improvement in the subject's situation.

CHAPTER 5

BORN TO BE BAD?

In which we develop the winning ways that entice people to our point of view

Employers often go off on tirades about 'attitude' or, more to the point, the 'poor attitude' of the people who should be tearfully grateful for the opportunity to work for them. This attitude thing has got so out of hand that, unbelievably, HR departments have started building in attitude as a qualification – or more frighteningly in some cases – as the only qualification. They say, "If you recruit people for their skill and they have a poor attitude you can't train for attitude. But if you recruit for attitude you can always train for a skill. So recruit for attitude, not skill!"

What rubbish. What, I ask you, is an 'attitude' and if you can tell me what it is, what gives people a bad one? It isn't possible, I suppose, that we might cause it?

Building His Vision

Many years ago I was managing a building project and I had three people working for me – two had been with me for years but one was new, young, very strange, and unsettling to be with. One day, I paid a surprise visit to the site. I walked up to the first guy and said, "What are you doing?"

"What am I doing, boss? Why I'm laying bricks. I'm a brick layer – Flemish Bond if you're interested!"

I went up to the second guy.

"Why are you here?"

"I'm here for ten pounds an hour!"

Finally I came to the weird unsettling kid.

"What are you doing?"

"What am I doing?" He fixed me with the gimlet stare of a true fanatic. "What am I doing?" his voice raised an octave. "I'm building a place where ill people can be made well. I'm building a place where the sick can be healed!"

WOW! Now that was an amazing way of looking at his job. It left me feeling stunned and just a bit humble. What a different way of looking at things. What a different... ATTITUDE!

Actually we had to fire him because we were building a petrol station.

Harness His Enthusiasm

OK, this may or may not be a true story but the point is that this guy's enthusiasm, however apocryphal, was misdirected because I had failed to tell him what he was doing. If I had sat down with him and explained what I was doing, what we were creating and what we were building I probably could have harnessed his passion and enthusiasm just as much for building a gas station as building a hospital. In the same way, if people with a diner, a shop, or any other business sit down with a cup of coffee and some doughnuts to explain their plans, hopes and passions, everyone involved can understand them, put some valuable input into them, and subsequently deliver profitable results. While we market busily to our customers we so often fail to market inside our organisations to our team. If you are reading this and you run a big company, then you have a team. If you have a small business, you have a team (maybe just friends and family but still a team), and if it's just you trying to persuade, you better be pretty sure you know where you're going and believe in it wholeheartedly. Considering that last statement, do I believe in every cause that I am called to persuade for?

Yes, I Believe

When I was a kid, I so loved an argument that if there was a debate I was quite happy to take any side and fight just as convincingly for whichever cause. So can I persuade for something I don't really believe in myself? What I actually did was, as I constructed my argument with its questions and evidence, I started to believe fiercely in it myself.

There are two ways to look at this. Either I am so persuasive that I can even convince a hard-bitten cynic like me, or I am a gullible halfwit. Whichever, if you can't convince yourself, then it is unlikely you can convince others. Next you must sell to, and forewarn, those around you about what you have been leading people to expect so that they can deliver it on your behalf.

Perhaps this is the time to mention persuasive management. The first thing that you need to do is ensure that the people working with you clearly understand what is at the heart of what you are offering. This isn't a new idea and the HR and marketing departments have long searched for the holy grail of 'core values', 'mission statements', and 'company vision'. Why, then, wherever we go, do we get rotten service, disappointing experiences, and disloyal, miserable staff? For fun and amusement, take some faceless corporate giant (even a government department) and hunt for their mission statement. It will probably contain words like 'solutions', 'excellence', and 'values'. Something like, "By valuing our people we can strive for excellence by being the number one choice for logistical solutions." Actually, they are usually even more contrived than that but I haven't got the weird brain needed to construct such balderdash.

Your task, when you have found said statement, is to find an employee and ask them:

(a) if they can repeat the mission statement;

(b) if they understand it; and

(c) are they permitted to deliver it.

My new car breaks down. "I am not happy, Give me a new car!" ... pointing to the mission statement which reads, "Empowering our people to delight our customers through dedication to doing whatever it takes to give total satisfaction."

"I can't give you a new car; it's more than my job's worth. It isn't my job to make those sort of decisions. You will have to write to Head Office."

Timeout

Here we go again, contradictions that cause confusion and disappointment.

Humour often works most sharply when there is a fair bit of fear and darkness. Recently I have watched a very dark TV comedy called 'Psychoville' (the title alone should alert you). Two characters that got me laughing from where I was hiding behind the sofa are children's entertainers, both clowns, one called Mr Jolly and the other Mr Jelly. One had been an orthopedic surgeon who wanted to be a clown and was so jealous of the other's success that he contrived to amputate his hand and steal his identity.

So we have the figure of a child's entertainer who is a clown with an iron hook, total despair, and a bad drink problem. Yes, it is really funny but I suppose you have to be there. It is funny because of the contradiction. What isn't funny is if your enterprise collapses because of your contradictions.

♩ Don't advertise the best coffee in the town if it isn't.

◡ Don't show up at a job interview a bit smelly and unprepared.

◡ Don't make promises that you can't deliver.

Stating The Bleedin' Obvious

In my recent TV series I went into failing businesses and helped to put them straight. The show was well received but the most telling comment came from a daily newspaper critic who didn't like the show. He said, "Geoff Burch just wanders into these businesses, states the bleedin' obvious, and then wanders out again!"

Yep, that's exactly what I did, and after doing it most of the businesses experienced a turnaround in their fortunes. Why couldn't they see the 'bleedin' obvious' for themselves?

Another business guru came up with a brilliant analogy he called 'The Ugly Baby' syndrome. In other words, a chum shows you their baby who is so ugly it could stop a clock. You don't tell them it is ugly, you don't tell them the truth, you say, "What a tough little guy. I bet he will grow up to be a footballer."

The fact is that it is very difficult to get the truth, especially from people who know us and love and care for us, but we do have to get it because on our persuasion road map we have to know exactly where we are with no flannel or flattery.

Passion Fruit

Back, then, to our people. Forget the mission and vision stuff, at the heart of what you are doing there is something you truly believe in. Maybe it's a passion or a dream. When you were a kid, the night before your birthday or Christmas or a party you would be so excited that you couldn't sleep. If you started a business, met someone you fancied, or were beginning a new job, you would be just as excited: the dreams you would have, the plans for the future, and the great ideas you would implement. In your head today, despite being worn down with routine, problems and fatigue, those enthusiasms are still there. Fish them out, dust them off, re-sell them to yourself … and then get out the coffee and those dough-nuts again, surround yourself with all your people, and sell those passions of yours to them. Once they understand that passion, they have a very simple choice to make. They can either be Ambassadors or Assassins. Do you really want to employ assassins? It is rare to find a person who gets true job satisfaction from being awful. "I had a great day at work today. I was truly crap!"

But they do exist. I hate to fire people but there is even a persuasive nice way of doing that when every other avenue has been explored. I watched an American friend the other day do the horrible deed:

"John, you are such a lovely guy and it really wakes people up when you scamper around the store naked, but I think you will be so much happier working some place else!"

Choose Your Attitude

Yes, it is great to employ people with a great attitude, but understand what an attitude actually is. It is not something we are born with. Attitude is the behaviour we CHOOSE for ourselves.

When we get up in the morning and that miserable crea-ture stares back at us from the mirror, we can there and then choose not to be like that. If people work for you, why should they choose a behaviour that is helpful to you? You can, by persuasion, change attitudes.

First Day at Work

What was your first day at work like? Were you greeted by surprise that you were even there?

"Oh! You're, um, you're the new, er (looking at watch…) um…now I've got a meeting so we'll find someone to, er…(looking frantically around until a character is spotted scratching its bottom) Terry – you aren't doing anything, show…thingy here the ropes!"

Terry enquires of you, "You new here, are you?"

"Yes!" you reply, eager to please.

"It's crap working here!" Terry helpfully advises. "If you ever want to steal anything, chuck it over the fence at the back. You can collect it later when he's too drunk to notice."

My company did a bit of research on staff dishonesty, particularly in retail, and some of the till fiddles are astonishingly sophisticated. One, I believe, was called 'Ringing the Changes'. It involves a good understanding of the cash register's mechanics and quite superior skills in mental arithmetic. It must have taken a genius to originally work that one out and then very willing, enthusiastic and attentive students to carry it forward to virtually every store in the land. If only our training could be that effective.

Kevin Goes to Zurich

The way we treat people has an astonishing effect on them. If you see what you perceive to be a dim, feckless youth, how do you think you could persuade him to be a hardworking, motivated, loyal employee? Can I suggest that, rather than talk at him, that we could look to ourselves and choose a behaviour set for ourselves that would transform him.

Close to us, there is a huge mill that employs many people but the only access to it is via a narrow bridge. It was young Kevin's first day in his first ever job. He had left school early because he was not the sharpest knife in the box and was trudging over the bridge pushing his bicycle. A large chauffeur-driven Rolls Royce glided to a halt next to him, one of the rear darkened windows slid down and a cultured voice spoke to him from the interior.

"Hello. Who are you?"

"I'm Kevin," came the reply after some period of reflection.

"Haven't seen you before. Do you work here?"

"Yeah, it's my first day."

"Do you know who I am?" enquired the voice.

"No".

"I am Sir Gordon Miles. I own this place. Do you have a passport?"

This one has really foxed Kevin, but after some thought it is one question he can answer. "Yes, my mum took me to Lanzarote for me holidays!"

"Jolly good! You pop home and get it," said the voice. "I have decided that you should spend your first day with me and we have to take the company jet to Zurich for a meeting."

Can you imagine the scene when he got home from his first day to be greeted by his mum?

"Hello, Mum!"

"How's your first day, our Kevin," and noticing the slightly late hour, "where have you been?"

Reply…"Zurich!"

Kevin was a loyal employee from that day forward and never forgot his day with the chief executive in Zurich.

We spend a fortune on recruitment and training and then fall at the first hurdle. You know the person is coming to work for you, you know they need a desk, a chair, a cup, someone to have lunch with. That person will probably bond with them for their whole career so why put them with someone dodgy?

The Dirty Dog

There is a story that I have put in all my books so I won't repeat the whole thing along with the barking and howling, but quite simply it is about someone trying to house-train a dog. Every time the dog does a poo in the house he beats the dog and throws it out of the window. This goes on for days and then weeks of poos, beatings, and window ejections. The dog doesn't seem to learn anything until one day it rushes into the house, does yet another poo on the carpet…and then jumps out of the window. I meet so many bosses who make exactly this mistake.

"Since we introduced flogging for anybody caught stealing we have not caught anyone pilfering."

"So, the stealing's stopped, then?"

"No. We just haven't caught anyone, that's all!"

This isn't the psychology bit of the book just yet but we must examine some very fundamental psychology at this point.

Let's look at a very simple route to persuasion.

Ↄ You would like to persuade someone to do something for you (just humour me, please, right now with a bit of a think). If you could persuade anyone to do anything, who would that person be and what would you persuade them to do? Look, you picked up this book because you felt you would like persuasion skills but if you can't pick a target there isn't much point, is there?

Ↄ You ask that person to do what you want them to do. (This is the second hurdle we all fall at because it is very rare in our day-to-day life that we ever ask anyone to do anything.) More of this later, but perhaps you are reading this because you make things and you feel it would be nice if people bought those things from you. Here is a simple, easy-to-master little technique. Walk up to your target and say, "Please buy my things!" A surprising number will say "yes" which will make you rich. Of course, many will say "no" and that is where the next bit comes in.

Ↄ People who resist what we would like them to do are in fact displaying a type of behaviour. It is a behaviour that involves them not doing what we want. (By the way, that is why step two was so important, because if you didn't clearly ask them for something, how do you know they are resisting? They may well have just been waiting to be asked).

The posh name for this is 'behaviour modification'. Let's look at the unruly dog. The beating and fear of beating did succeed in modifying its behaviour but in a most negative and unpredictable way (actually, entirely predictable but wholly undesirable). We train the dog to avoid the beating, we train thieving staff to become more sly and circumspect, and we train the bullied customer to lie about their intentions. "Well, that seems lovely. I'll pop back in a day or two and pick one up!" "I've just got to run this by my partner!" "I'll just think it over!"

So what do we do with the dog? Well, it's in its nature to poo anywhere which means that it is almost certainly going to also do it where we want – say in the garden. When it does, we should rush over with biscuits, praise, and loads of love. In other words it's our job to **catch people doing things right**! Praise, smiles, and approval are all great behaviour modifiers. For example, the customer has bought from you but has taken the cheaper option:

"Boy, you have got yourself a great bargain. You are really going to enjoy using it!"

Taking a rewarding attitude and congratulating the customer will make them want to repeat the experience time and time again and you have got a customer for life. The point is that choosing rewarding behaviours in yourself is one of the most powerful persuasive tools you can use. Again, catch them doing something right!

Play Nicely, Now!

Hang on, am I being rumbled here? You've just invested all this time to learn the secrets of persuasion and get to this point only to find that I am saying one of the best ways to persuade people is to be nice to them? Truthfully, this is one of the most important and powerful persuasion techniques. The first and most successful book on persuasion was *How to Win Friends and Influence People*. Dale Carnegie, in a sort of 'mom, apple pie, corn cob pipe puffing on the porch' sort of way, intuitively realised that people would become putty in your hands if you were nice to them.

The psychologists now would describe it as using positive strokes – things like the use of the person's name, appreciating and praising their attributes, possessions and skills, using the appropriate and respectful appearance and body language, listening skills and good eye contact. These all make people feel good and because people are always eager to feel even good-er, they will do anything for you if being around you makes them have good feelings.

Whenever we have any contact with another person there is one of three states that we can leave them in:

- ✓ **NEGATIVE.** This is where they part from us feeling worse than they did when they met us. You queue for hours in some office for the official to tell you that you have filled in the form all wrong, you are dumb, and you will have to wait a week before you can try again.
- ✓ **NEUTRAL.** The middle way that most of us get. The transaction between two people that leaves us with no feelings one way or the other "Burger and fries, please." You get them, you leave. Anything memorable, distinctive, any changes in your emotions? Didn't think so.
- ✓ **POSITIVE.** This is where you leave feeling better than when you started. The big sunny smile, the other person telling you genuinely how nice it is to see you, and using the name you like to be called by (not the pizza restaurant 'hi guys' which makes me want to fly at them).

Behaviour That Changes Behaviour

My wife is a much more sensitive and attuned person than I am and you would do much better to follow her example in this area. We had suffered an appalling journey of traffic jams, delayed flights, and quite vigorous domestic disputes. Arriving late at our hotel, dishevelled, tired, and dispirited, we were told by the cheery desk clerk that they didn't have a room ready for us. We were too tired to even fight back so, crushed by this final straw; we flopped in the lounge in sullen silence until summoned by the clerk some while later, who told us the room was now ready. We arrived at the room just in time to see a trolley-pushing chambermaid leaving. She looked like a cross between James Bond's Rosa Clebb and a troll. My wife was first into the newly prepared room and then a split second later she was first out! Just as the troll was disappearing round a corner in the corridor, my wife called to her: "Please stop, just a moment!" The troll stopped. "Did you just prepare this room?"

The troll stood firm as their eyes locked. "Yep!"

I was, by this time, looking around for safe cover as the missus continued:

"We have been travelling for thirteen hours non-stop. We are tired, dirty, and exhausted. We arrived at this hotel to find the room not ready. Then, when I walked into it, I found fresh flowers, clean fragrant bed linen, a spotless bathroom, and even a choccy on my pillow. What a fabulous job you have done. I am sure you do hundreds of rooms just as nicely but I had to tell you that you have saved my day. You are a superstar! Thank you so much."

The troll froze, and then little by little, bits of craggy face started to move and rearrange itself into the biggest smile I had ever seen. She went off pushing her trolley with what appeared to be little skips and I even caught her smiling at the other guests and asking if she could get them anything. I knew the 'girl had dun' good' because every night after that we were the only couple to get two chocs on our pillows! Of course at the end of our stay a modest tip changed hands, but it wasn't the money that had won the day, it was the positive behaviour towards another person that had been the cause of the positive behaviour in return.

Make 'Em Smile, Make 'Em Smile

Here is your exercise. You will, over the course of the next few days or so, encounter all sorts of people – taxi drivers, work colleagues, family, and strangers. Whatever interaction you have with them will either leave them feeling reduced (negative), neither up nor down (neutral), or feeling better for having met you (positive). Try, just for this experiment, to always go for the positive. Start small. When you pass people on the street, give them a warm smile – a huge percentage of the time they will smile back. Fact: people who are smiling are happier than people who aren't; therefore you just made a complete stranger happy.

Next, try a bit harder to find something about the other person, how they look, or what they are doing, that you can make a positive comment about. Tell the taxi driver how skilful and professional his driving is, tell a work colleague how much their cheeriness brightens up the day. Clearly the teenager with the shiny motor scooter is as proud as punch with it – admire it, tell him how you wish that you had the freedom of the open road.

This might appear too obvious and too simple for you but what you are doing is changing peoples' behaviour. You are consciously altering events by choosing your behaviour too. That is control, and control is absolutely key to persuasion. It is so powerful that it can also be dangerous. The person you praise for being cheery will so love the feeling you gave them that they will never stop searching you out to be cheery to you. Oh, what fun to be the target of the office cheery person! The kid with the motorbike, if told how much you admire his vim, vigour, and courage, will roar away with his front wheel pawing the air and in all likelihood will break his neck. So, simply by making conscious changes to what you do, you change the world.

POINTS TO PONDER ON CHAPTER 5

1. People can be unexpectedly wonderful but we do have to direct their energies in the right direction by explaining to them clearly what we want them to do.

2. No one is born with a bad attitude - in fact there is no such thing as an attitude. It is simply a behaviour that they choose for themselves. What you do to people helps them to choose.

3. If you know someone new is going to come and work with you, if you make it the most special day of their life, you could create lifelong loyalty.

4. You can alter anyone's behaviour by choosing behaviours for yourself that will change them.

5. Always try and leave everybody you meet with positive feelings - they will love you for it.

6. One of the biggest modifiers of people's behaviour is to always try and catch them doing things right. Punishment can change them but not always in the way you expect.

CHAPTER **6**

VERY INTERESTED

In which we gather the vital information that gives us power

In the past, salespeople were terrified that they would waste a valuable presentation and therefore a lot of time on someone who would not – or even worse – could not give them a positive buying decision. They were both right and wrong about this. The tough sales manager would become apoplectic if he felt that one of his team had failed to speak to the 'decision maker' or because the hapless salesperson had failed to, 'Qualify' the 'Prospect'. So let's have a look at what's right before we get on to the next bit.

We have two big faults of human nature here, one on our side and one on the other person's side, but in a way it is driven by the same touch of paranoia. This is the desire to retain status, be loved and respected, while at the same time avoiding a fight, confrontation, or any other kind of similar unpleasantness. What that sales manager realized is that it is very easy to give a good, comfortable sales presentation to a cheery liar, who has no intention or means to buy. It might feel safer to come away with a promise of nothing, a smile and a warm handshake, rather than have an uncomfortable discussion with the subject where you learn about all of the flaws in your proposition. We are literally trained from birth, when we receive a smack on the chubby little hand that has reached out for the gas stove, to fear the word "No" and we will do anything to avoid it – even if it means being misled. The real persuader has to have the courage to mine down deep to get to the sometimes uncomfortable truth – which may even mean you have been talking to the wrong person.

V.Int

There is a phrase that I may repeat in this book that I never ever want you to use ever again and that is 'VERY INTERESTED!' No one is ever 'very interested'. If you are a buyer, never torment a salesperson with it and if you are a seller never put it in a progress report – or worse, the shortened, jaunty 'V.INT' because they aren't. Take my word for it. It's uncomfortableness time again but it has to be done.

Persuasion, by definition, is a confrontational art, the skill is to not make it appear so, but it is. Someone will believe one thing and when you have finished they will believe another. What they end up believing is what you have chosen for them to believe, and if you don't think that is a recipe for a bit of a dust up, it might be time to think again. First you need to find out what they believe. If it is entirely in line with what you want them to believe then there is no persuading to do.

Scene: The Greengrocer
"Do you have bananas?"
"Would you like some bananas?"
"Yes, I love bananas!"
"I have these bananas"
"They look good bananas. How much are they?"
"A pound a bunch!"
"Then I will take three bunches, please."

No persuasion there then. The minute the greengrocer asks, "What else can I get you?", the persuading from "Just bananas" can start. The problem is that people lie to avoid the problem of pre-persuasion confrontation and the persuader plays along because they want to avoid confrontation too.

The Time-Waster's Guide

One boring Sunday afternoon, you and your partner decide to while away a pleasant hour or two looking at those new super executive homes that they are building in the next town, complete with indoor pool and pony paddock. You stroll into the show home and out leaps the salesperson, uniformed, obsequious and fragrant. You will be treated to an orgy of politeness, attention, and respect; after all you are going to be spending a few million, aren't you? "The light switches are, of course, solid gold!"

"Very nice!" you murmur. "Who would want less."

"I'm sure you'll agree that the chauffeur's flat is as comfortable and spacious as the average family home."

"Well, you do have to keep the staff happy," you agree eagerly. I bet that person suspects you are just wasting time but in truth is unlikely to grab you by the throat, pin you to the wall, and say, "Listen, you time-wasting pillock, I think you are skint! Show me the money or get orf the site!" On the other side, we tend to get a bit twitchy about saying, "I could never afford a place like this but can I have a look around," because you may well be shown round but you won't get the champagne flute, or the nibbles, and the salesperson will probably polish every surface you dare to touch! But how did you behave when you did buy your house?

"Of course, the views are nice."

You reply, "The gas works rather spoil it."

"But it's well priced."

You reply, "It's far more than I wanted to spend."

The point is, you tend to be a lot more negative on occasions when you do buy than on occasions when you don't buy. Why would you bother to go to the trouble of upsetting somebody that you have no intention of buying from, but when it comes to spending your money, manners come a very poor second best?

Nice People Don't Buy

Why are you being so horrid? It is because you want to buy. The experienced salesperson can see that as part of the qualification process. What we need are some qualifying questions. Classically they would be things about budget, position, and urgency to buy. The problem is that it is easy to get into this lying conspiracy again.

"Well, shall we reserve this plot for you today?"

"I'm sure there will be no problem. We love this place but we just have to go and measure the pony so we'll probably pop back later to tie things up!"

Both parties here have emotionally escaped. We have escaped with our pride and a pocket full of nibbles; they get relief from the boredom of the Sunday shift and a 'V.Int' in the report sheet. The best questions to ask at this point are indirect ones.

"Can I get you a drink? What is your favourite wine?"

If the reply is "Cider", don't dismiss it but store it in your box of clues.

"How many children do you have? How nice! Where do they go to school?" Bash Street or Eton – in the clue box.

By asking people indirect questions, you will get them to inadvertently reveal much more than they would have done by direct questioning which could alert them to your motives.

You Can't Judge a Book by Looking at Its Cover

Be careful, you can make dreadful mistakes. There are always stories of mad millionaires who arrive with £20 notes in a dirty shoebox, but generally where the prospective buyer lives, where they work, what position they hold, what makes them choose to view your product should all go in the clue box. Treat them well, but when the clues add up don't write 'V.Int' because you are only fooling yourself. The motor trade calls these people tyre kickers or time wasters.

The Chimp and The Mercedes

Let me tell you a little story. When I was a youth, you could describe me as a chimp-like, biker type of teenager. I had a large, elderly, but very powerful motorcycle which, due to its age, had become incontinent and left little pools of oil everywhere. Our local Mercedes garage was famous for two things, its elegance and the world's toughest and most successful salesman – a person to be feared. A new Mercedes had just been launched at a lavish event. As a lover of all things mechanical I had to see this car so, as the local dignitaries enjoyed their chamber orchestra and canapes, I pressed my oily face against the window as a growing pool appeared under my bike. This notorious salesman saw me and came storming out. "What are you doing here?" "Came to see the car," was my reply. "You going to buy one, then, lad?" he said with a leer. "Could never afford one, I'm broke," I replied defiantly as I turned to leave.

"You will one day, boy. Here, take the keys of one and enjoy it for an hour or two, and I'll get one of the engineers to have a look at your bike while you're doing it."

Can you imagine how I felt – a kid of eighteen cruising round my hometown streets in a beautiful brand new Merc!

Over ten years later, I was in the same dealership ordering my first new Mercedes from this very salesman. All he said was, "I knew you'd be back!"

I think that was the first time anyone had shown any belief in my ability to achieve anything. Maybe, and only maybe, it was that little bit of belief that gave me the impetus to achieve Mercedes-owning earnings? You never know, but what was for sure was that the guy had realized that after qualifying you should never dismiss anyone as useless.

Everyone is Important

So, if we are to treat everyone the same, what are we qualifying them for? Once we find out what they can give us, then that is what we ask them for. Meeting anyone in life is never a waste of time. Qualifying allows you to understand what they know and how they can take you forward on your journey. Elsewhere in this book, we contemplate a journey to Alaska and in a rural village we meet a local resident. Through careful questioning it may be revealed that our rustic friend from Nether Wapping has no knowledge of North America at all, but he does know the way to the nearest highway after which you should thank him profusely, praise his local knowledge, and then ask him to give you directions.

Don't Let The Librarian Waste your Time

You have a meeting set up with a firm of architects to demonstrate your stressed concrete roof trusses and realize that you have got the office junior. I had a situation like this once where I was coaching a group who actually did visit architects. They would do a presentation of the benefit of the product range, and also explain a very expensive and well produced product selector – sort of catalogue thing. The point with architects is that they sometimes think that they are 'too cool for school' and feel it is beneath them to waste time speaking to salespeople. However, building design is a moving and changing discipline and architects really should meet manufacturers to understand the use and application of new materials. They get round this (in their heads, anyway) by appointing the most junior (and perceived), useless member of staff to be what they euphemistically call the 'Practice Librarian'. In other words, they gather up all the catalogues and literature, classify them, and store them for the designer to peruse for their next project.

I would ask these salespeople how they got on. "Fantastic! They were very interested!"

When asked what evidence they had of this 'V.Int' position, they would reply that they had done the whole 'dem' without interruption and shifted a full set of catalogues and a presenter file (costing my client hundreds of pounds). They seemed to feel that the more of these they shifted, the greater evidence of their 'hard work'. In this case, why are we speaking to this person? Some simple qualifying questions would have revealed their lowly status.

"What project are you currently working on?"

"Have you personally specified a similar product to this?"

When we look in our evidence box we can see it is time to change tack. What do we want? We need to move up the food chain to someone who is in a position to specify our product. The chances are that won't happen today but what is the most the person we are with capable of giving us? They have a lot of inside knowledge so let's ask for that.

"I suppose the senior partner must be near retirement age. Who do you reckon will succeed him?" "Everyone seems busy – have you got a new project on the go?" And of course he could introduce you to his boss – not subtle at this stage, but why not ask...

"His name's John Smith? I would love to meet him. Would you introduce us, please?"

Worth a shot!

This chapter is not about whether you are talking to the right person or the wrong person, but is about understanding the person you are talking to and getting to the truth. If you are not getting genuine information because either the other person is misleading you or, worse still, you are misleading yourself, you will never know where you are on this routemap to persuasion.

POINTS TO PONDER ON CHAPTER 6

1. If the person you are trying to persuade agrees with everything you say, be suspicious. People who are genuinely being persuaded often have reservations and, if they are really interested, aren't afraid to express them.

2. Persuasion is about changing people's minds. If they know what they want and they buy what they want, you haven't exactly persuaded them.

3. Asking indirect questions can tell you a lot that the person didn't want to reveal. For instance, whether they are the right person you should be talking to or if you need to change your offer to appeal to their hidden side.

4. Whilst we don't always talk to the decision maker, remember everybody can make decisions that can be helpful.

5. Nobody is ever, ever 'very interested'.

CHAPTER 7

THE TOUGH OLD MONSTERS OF SALES

In which we discover the powerful sales techniques that can still work their magic for us now

Now that we are sure we are qualified to win opportunities, we know that the promises and expectations we have generated can be fulfilled or even exceeded. Our appearance has been carefully manipulated and selected to ensure that it in no way contradicts our promise, and that every aspect of the way we look raises our personal capital. We have chosen a set of rewarding behaviours that will fundamentally alter the way the other person behaves. If you can tick off every point on that checklist, then you are ready to persuade. You are well equipped to start the journey of persuasion.

But we are only at base camp staring up at the summit. All of this meticulous preparation only gives us the opportunity, but the opportunity to do what?

To turn our journey theme on its head for a moment, whilst it is a useful analogy to suggest that our adventure in persuasion is a sort of journey and to make it succeed we need to know where we are, by the same token we are taking the object of our persuasion on a journey and we need to know where they are. This is particularly relevant when it comes to sales persuasion which, I may suggest, is becoming a bit of a lost art. At its extreme, the sales journey would be from, "I hate you and I would never buy one" to "Yes please, I will buy two!" This requires a major change in the person's frame of mind to say the least.

A Tough Old Game

Selling is a tough old game, and in the old days it was required that one was fully loaded with 'selling skills'. This meant that sales trainers strode the earth like superstars as their books became best sellers. Although clearly dinosaurs, is there anything from them that we can use in our sophisticated modern world?

I have just picked up a book called *A Thousand Ways to Increase your Sales* with some great tips such as: Always remove your hat when talking to a buyer; Keep your bus tickets to show your manager; and, most useful of all, Be cautious selling to women because they are governed by their likes and dislikes! We give a little chuckle. But this smug enjoyment of our complacent third-wayism came down with a bit of a bump the other day.

They Had Never Sold Anything in their Lives

At the time of writing this, the world is in a huge financial turmoil, and no more so than in the building industry. Recently I was summoned to be the keynote speaker at one of Europe's biggest house builder's sales conferences. The audience, unsurprisingly, were the sales force. These people, hundreds of them, were having a torrid time because of the housing crash. Should I talk about selling the benefits? Perhaps putting on a killer demonstration could be selling the finance package... But then I saw my audience, battered, bewildered, lost, and mostly under thirty years of age. All they had ever seen was boom, the feeding frenzy that had been the housing hysteria – the fish had just jumped into their boat. Despite their title, they had never had to sell anything in their lives. Their selling was to lurk in a show home and when the punters arrived, the sales pitch was,

"Hello."

"Hello! Can I have this house please?"

"No, they are all sold. Leave a deposit and I will put your name down for phase two."

"Thank you, you are an angel."

"No problem. Now get lost, I'm reading the sports pages."

Extinct?

A provocative statement may be that we owe our current financial crisis to the fact that nobody can sell any more. Before Ford and GM had their troubles, the roads swarmed with their product all being driven by sales representatives in pursuit of orders for their companies. In those days the western world actually made things, it bought raw materials and components and then added value by some industrial process before selling it on at a profit to someone else. The companies who made components and raw materials would send out armies of sales people to win the battle for orders.

Here is a very harsh snapshot of life back then. Four salespeople would have an appointment to see a buyer of components. After each one did their best to show their product in the best light, only one would walk out with the order. For every purchase made, there were always a number of disappointed salespeople. It was usual to have more supply than demand. The empty-handed salesperson could cost his company jobs. The winner put food on everyone's table so it is no wonder they became superstars.

Well, those times are back.

A street has five coffee bars – why should people drink in yours? Five window cleaners called this week, why should I use you? You make garden furniture but so do five hundred other people. Why should I buy from you?

Selling Quality

The other result of the death of the salesperson is that, as the public, we have started to buy rubbish. Let's make one thing very clear – the early salesperson had it drummed into them, "Never sell on price." That one-in-four salesperson who got orders by slashing prices would soon finish his employer off.

A Head of Steam

I love to build small steam engines and the key piece of kit in the steam engine builder's armoury is a metal working lathe. Industry would describe this as a machine tool. The West's machine tool industry has been decimated for pretty obvious reasons. An American or European small lathe may cost £10,000, but a Chinese copy can be bought for £1000. They don't work that well and some of the metal they are made from is a bit like cheese, but they are getting better. When you type 'Model making lathe' into the internet, up pops the Wan-kee Lathe company, probably renamed and marketed by a Western importer under the Truprecise brand or some such thing.

Lurking in the centre of England is a factory of elves that still makes a slightly old-fashioned traditional lathe. They are very expensive even though the elves don't make much money but I have acquired a second hand one. Oh what joy, what bliss! It is like the difference between supermarket chocolate yoghurt and Raymond Blanc's hand-folded Belgium chocolate mousse. The old salespeople used to say, "You only cry once when you buy quality!" The problem is that we, as customers, don't buy quality any more because no one knows how to sell it.

In The Steps of The Master

Let's have a look at how the old timers used to do it. I make no apologies for their oiliness, lack of political correctness, or perceived pushiness. They got the job done – we can do subtle later. I will also try and put the complete sale here even though it might short-circuit our journey a bit because the traditional sales techniques do need to be seamless, from "Hello" to "Sign here, please."

One feature of the early sales teams, caused by the fact that companies couldn't afford to carry passengers, meant that the new recruits were thrown in at the deep end and were expected to come back with orders. There was no career development, just a big stick. For this reason, the 'steps of the sale' as they called it were often broken down in acronyms and formulas. All these, when listed, will elicit a sigh of despair from the cognoscenti who will say, "Not that old stuff again. We've done all that!" They may have done, but to make these systems work you needed nerve, persistence, and hard work – something that I am sure all of us would like to avoid if we could. If you haven't seen this stuff before, the science of it works, and if you can grit your teeth and forget your modesty it will work for you.

It's Only Words

Let's just examine the vocabulary. The person you are going to persuade is called the 'Prospect' because until they buy something there is only a prospect of business. They are not customers until they buy, they are prospects. Looking for them is called 'prospecting'. If you hear of a likely 'prospect' that is a 'lead'. If you know they want to buy, that is a 'hot lead'. If it is just a name which fits your usual customer profile, that would be called a 'cold lead'. If you take a list of names of likely customers and just call to sell unannounced, that is called 'cold calling' or even 'on the knocker'. If it is to generate 'leads', that is called 'canvassing'. If you have turned a 'prospect' into a 'customer' you

79

should always ask them to recommend others who would like what you have to offer. This is called 'asking for referrals'.

If you are experienced in sales I bet you think all this is a bit dumb, but just think for a moment and just look at the strength of intent and purpose there. When was the last time you dared to ask for a referral? When canvassing, do we forget the sole object is to get a hot lead for a time when the selling process can be conducted properly?

The Magic Formula

The sales process of presentation then takes place, following the steps of, sometimes patented, formulae. It is like a sort of bullfight that requires a bit of ole-ing, provoking, and pase doble-ing until the moment is felt to be right for the coup de grâce. The end! The sale! This is called the 'close', thought to be the most difficult and skilful moment, the one that only the finest toreadors of sales could accomplish clearly. In fact companies would advertise – not for salespeople, but for good closers. There are 'closing techniques' during the presentation. You could ask 'trial closes' such as, "When you take delivery of your shiny new car, Mr Peters, where would you drive to first?" (By the way, I hid an 'assumption close' in there as well.) This is like sticking a fork in the pie to see if it is done. Of course, during this battle, the 'prospect' will put up a bit of a fight. If the prospect says, "No, clear off or I'll call the police", that may suggest all is lost so we must ask questions that cannot elicit that fatal, "no". These are called open questions – Who, What, Why, When, Where, Which, How. This is why shop assistants are not supposed to say, "Can I help you", but instead, "How can I help you", so that you can't say no. Actually we develop a sort of deafness of convenience and still say, "No thanks, I'm just looking", but don't dismiss it totally out of hand. It does work if you have a small restaurant – there is a big difference between, "Do you want a table" and "Where would you like to sit?"

The questions that get yes or no are called 'say no' or 'closed' questions, but they do have a very powerful use for checking and strengthening resolve.

"You say you are tired of being burgled?"

"Yes."

"Do you want to stop them in their tracks?"

"Yes."

"Would you like the same fatal effects on all unwelcome visitors, say, your mother-in-law?"

"Yes!"

"Then let's go ahead and order the Acme Man Trap today!"

No Objections

Still the prospect is not in the bag and their struggles and resistance are referred to as 'objections'. (I really do have an issue with this one but let's examine this type of persuasion, warts and all, for now.) The accepted logic is, if they don't buy because of their objections, the removal or negation of those objections will mean they have to buy. This is called 'dealing with objections'. Once all the objections have been dealt with, the 'prospect' starts to exhibit another strange crop of symptoms which are called 'buying signals'. Perversely, buying signals can be expressed as objections and some objections are unspoken and exhibit a positive behaviour. For example, these can be, "Yes, that all seems great. I'll go away and think about it!" ("think about it", to a salesperson, is like garlic to a vampire). Now, if you think you are hard enough, you can uncover the objection and then nail it, but it takes some nerve and the hide of a rhinoceros.

"I'm glad you like it, but when someone says to me they want to think it over, they must have something to think about. That means there is something they are not sure about. What is it that I have failed to explain that you are not sure about and you need to think over?"

Would you dare to do that? It works, but the pressure is really on.

"Well, I think we have to see if we can afford it."

"If I could show you not only how to afford it, but how you could save money by ordering today, would you go ahead?"

See! The closed question is used to tie the prospect down. Tough stuff, I am sure you will agree. You do agree, don't you? What is it you are not sure about? See, you've got me doing it now.

POINTS TO PONDER ON CHAPTER 7

1. Just because the old guys used to do it doesn't mean it won't work now.

2. Just because your customers buy things - or used to buy things - doesn't mean you know how to sell. All it means is you failed to prevent them from spending their money.

3. If people aren't persuaded to buy good things they tend to buy rubbish.

4. People only cry once when they buy quality.

5. Always use open questions when you persuade and only ever use closed questions if you want to tie the other party down.

6. It takes courage to ask people to buy things. Have you got it?

CHAPTER **8**

WHEN I'M CALLING YOU

In which we discover how sales calls, finding leads and using old school methods are still powerful in today's business environment

If you watched a merchant selling whips, harnesses, and rocks to the Pharaohs, you would probably recognize some classic business techniques that we use today. Just because something is old doesn't mean that it is not valid in today's market. What we need to do is understand how the old sales techniques worked, why just a very few of them perhaps don't work and, more importantly, how – with a bit of modification and modernization – they can be just as powerful for us as they were for our predecessors, if only just to grant us an opportunity to present our case to the subject. There is no more powerful example of this than the probably mis-named 'telephone selling'; I suppose it would be a bit of a mouthful to say "telephone opportunity-getting" but that's what it really is.

Johnny Kaminski

Many years ago when I was starting my training company, I recruited an assistant. We used to sit in the office with few clients and very little work to do. Yes, I know we were supposed to show people how to sell, but they do say that the cobbler's children go worst shod. Finally, after a period of finger tapping and window staring my assistant said, "What we need is one of those really butch American salesmen – I bet he could get us appointments!"

Step forward Johnny Kaminski.

I was a sales expert and I know how these slick guys work, how they get past the gatekeeper, how they dangle carrots, arouse the interest, and secure the appointment – all on the telephone. It's just that at that time I didn't actually have the courage to try it. From that conversation we created this fictional character called Johnny Kaminski who had a pantomime American accent. We started to ring people with me using the voice of Johnny, my alter ego. There was no excess of ghastly pushiness that he wouldn't go to.

"Hi, honey! Who am I speaking to?"

"Janet!"

"Well hi, Janet. That's a real pretty name." (I know, I know, puke-making but stay with me.)

"Janet, I wonder if you could help me today." (Complete silence for some time – minutes, if it had to be, until Janet finally breaks the silence with an embarrassed giggle.)

"Tee hee, with what?"

"Well, honey," (yes, he really did call her honey), "thank you so much for asking. Who, right there, is in charge of training?"

More silence.

"Mr Jackson, I think."

"Mr Jackson, hey? Is he there right now?" (Watch every word, Johnny doesn't waste them and chooses them to have the most effect.)

"Yes, I believe he is."

"That's terrific. Would you put me through to him right now, please?"

"Can I tell him what it is about?"

"Sure, Janet. Tell him I've got a great oppor-tooonity for him!"

More of the long silence…

"Jackson!"

"Oh, Mr Jackson, it's Kaminski…Johnny Kaminski here. I'm so excited to be speaking to you today. Boy, have I got a great oppor-toooonity for you!"

It's too soon right now to show the whole speech and I bet you think that Johnny's patter well and truly grates. We did too, but he was a caricature created in a moment of boredom. To our amazement he broke through almost every time despite the ghastliness – his tidal wave of ebullience seemed to sweep all before him and almost inevitably he was offered an appointment.

Johnny Under The Microscope

Let's just take the above as a study subject. The key point that needs to be made is that Johnny succeeded in making appointments (which we subsequently never followed up because we didn't have the nerve or ability to continue the Johnny Kaminski thing face-to-face – I learned those skills later!). But first it will do no harm to examine Johnny's methods. He uses loads of questions and always waits for an answer. He knows that in selling, the first one to speak loses. He can turn around clichéd phrases and sayings from the other person to his own advantage because his target has spoken without thinking and consequently they are putty in his hands.

"Can I help you?" is the usual greeting.

"You sure can!" Silence until the other crumbles.

When we mortals want to speak to someone, our natural inclination is to ask, "Can I speak to Mr X, please?" The gatekeeper, secretary, or receptionist finds it easy and comfortable to be truthful and can truthfully say, "No" because even if he is there he doesn't want to be bothered. If, however, the question is, "Is Mr X there?" then the truthful answer must be "Yes" and the person is already in deep water.

Pushy But Proud

In many books that I have read recently about persuasion, sales, and negotiating skills, the authors have all been at pains to point out that theirs is a gentle art and they decry the foot-in-the-door, pushy, high pressure people of the bad old days. The trouble is that it worked. There are fabulous modern psychological techniques that are powerful, subtle instruments, but sometimes kicking the door in will get you what you want. Turning our backs on all the old ways is like throwing all the hammers out of the tool box – of course, careful work with an eyeglass, scalpel, and jeweler's screwdriver is satisfying but sometimes you have just got to whack it with a hammer. The cognoscenti would describe the early pushy salespeople as coarse and uncouth, lacking in finesse and completely stupid. Dinosaurs or sharks. Point taken! I'm sure that in political discourse, Tyrannosaurus Rex would be at a loss. The tricky problem of quantum mechanics and string theory would baffle Jaws, but when it comes to rending flesh with sharp powerful teeth we would come a poor and partially digested second. The useful lesson we can learn is that these creatures are built for a purpose – the shark is the perfectly engineered swimming and killing machine. Sure it has a tiny brain that has two simple jobs to do which are to control swimming and eating, and that's what it does best all day, every day. I don't think they even sleep as their streamlined form glides swiftly forward towards their next meal which could well be you, and if it is you, you don't stand a chance.

In life you are going to meet competitors like that, competitors for your lover, for your job, or for your customers. You may start your day considering life in other galaxies, maybe the drudgery of the day might make you stare from the window and calculate your carbon footprint as the drive home slows to a crawl, or a delicious crayfish recipe may pop into your head. Be warned, as you take your eye off the ball, a silent grey form with half your intellect but fifty times as many teeth is gliding up behind you. Being a bit thick is actually no handicap in the persuasion game because one of the simplest and most effective ways of getting what you want is with persistence. If you make ice cream, with no subtlety or planning you could walk up to people and say, "Buy an ice cream." It's a fact of life that a percentage will buy so by going on and on doing that for ever you will make a living. Ice cream be blowed – don't sell anything at all, just ask for the money!

It Beggars Belief

In my home town we have sorry looking beggars who sit out in all weathers simply saying, "Spare any change, please?" My sympathy for them was a little tempered when a survey was published which suggested that they earned an average of £30,000 a year. Are you a research scientist who has started a genetic engineering laboratory? Is this your second year? Are you pleased to have broken even? Well, my local tramp makes more than you do.

Keep It Simple, Stupid!

This functions particularly well when you find a formula that works. I met a multi-millionaire recently who I really felt was possibly a few sandwiches short of a picnic. He manufactured a basic confectionary product that he found sold really well in railway or bus stations, so he went round the world opening kiosks in bus and railway stations.

"Why don't you expand your product range or try different locations?" I asked. He looked at me as if I had suggested bestiality, cannibalism or country dancing. I could have been telling a tyrannosaurus to take up basket weaving!

The problem for us mere mortals is boredom. If I told you that the best way to get new business would be to get the telephone directory and ring everyone in it from A to Z, at around 'Aardvark' you would be getting a tiny bit fatigued.

Again, I'm going to upset the new world, reform persuader (me included) by suggesting that scripts may be a good thing.

Stick to The Script

I work with a lot of tough-minded, direct selling and multi-level marketing people who have, by the pressure of constant rejection, a large turnover of naïve team members. They have created a script that works in a known percentage of cases – say seven in every hundred calls. Make five hundred calls and sell thirty five. I would rather duck and weave, fire from the hip, react and interact. I feel I could do better than seven percent but if you've never done it before and all you want is the opportunity to use your other skills to earn a living, then get a script and use it *ad nauseam*.

Full Steam Ahead

I will talk for a moment more about steam engines. As I have already said, in my spare time I build (very badly) small steam locomotives. Actually, on reflection, they are quite large; they are coal-fired and can pull people round a track. When fresh plans arrive I dream in a cloud of sooty steam of pulling up an incline with my engine driver's hat on. I go to my metal stock pile and pull out a large plate of shiny steel. Then I start to drill holes, holes for the rivets, holes for the pipes, holes for the bearings, thousands and thousands of holes. I dive in with cheery enthusiasm but after the first four hundred I am so bored, so horribly bored. My workshop is full of hole-ridden metal that has been abandoned in a fugue of fatigue, and I have achieved nothing.

Boredom is the biggest threat we face to making us abandon possibly lucrative or fulfilling projects. Just grit your teeth and get on with it. To succeed like Johnny Kaminski you must develop some level of mindless persistence. The water drip can bore (in every sense of the word) through solid granite. My point is that we view the distant peaks which are our destination with enthusiasm but actually that destination is achieved by the drudgery of single footsteps.

If It Works, Repeat It, for Repeated Success!

The next big lesson we can learn from Johnny is confidence. Of course we were play-acting but we were play-acting the part of someone who was very self-assured and confident. If, for any reason, we are not confident, the other party can literally smell the fear and things can go swiftly pear-shaped. Let's go together to a darkened room, lie on my couch with a cool cloth on your forehead and tell me what it is you are not confident about. Is it that the promises you are making about the future aren't true? Maybe you sell home improvements that you know are a rip-off. There is nothing more confidence sapping than knowing a success-ful sale could result in a baying lynch mob. What's that you say? You believe your offer is fabulous and can't be bettered? So why the nerves?

Hot Leads

A famous old sales story concerned a man who had gone to work in the tough world of commission-only insurance sales. In this game the true gold is to have a list of people you know are interested called 'Leads' or, if very interested, 'Hot leads'. These are hard and expensive to come by and are generated by recommendation, bird dogs, advertising, and telephone canvassing. If one goes shooting, there is a dog that can point out the birds. In selling, a 'bird dog' is someone like a barber, a bartender, or a coffee-shop owner who you give a modest payment to so that they will heart-ily recommend your business at every opportunity and to everyone they meet. The leads are therefore very parsimoni-ously shared out and are often given to the star salesper-son to avoid wasting these treasures. A rare and valuable creature is a salesperson that can generate their own leads, but this guy was a true tyro and was becoming dispirited. In this game, staff retention is hard, so to give this guy a break the boss gave him ten hot leads; even with his lack of skill, he managed to turn four of them into definite sales. Untrained and unsubtle he said, "I'm sorry to bother you but I understand you need insurance." When he came back to the office he begged for ten more leads which reluctantly he was given. He came back again and again until the boss grew tired and threw the telephone directory to him saying, "Get them from there! That's where I've been getting them from all along!"

They weren't hot at all, but the belief that they were had generated the confidence. It's bad enough when our target does say "no" without us doing it in our heads on their behalf!

The Confidence Trick

So, let's just have a look at your confidence checklist. Let's, for this exercise, assume that you need to make as many appointments as possible on the telephone – one job that I personally hate and which leaves me in bits. The problem is that I can't decide whether it is the boredom (as in drilling holes) or the fear that screws me up. I suppose it's a bit like defusing bombs – very dull just unscrewing bolt after bolt until you unscrew the wrong one which leaves bits of you festooned around the surrounding trees. It's the perfect analogy because, whilst dull and repetitive, any exciting moments could be terminal. In other words, keep your wits about you. There are no second chances on offer.

For some inspiration, let us once again look at the old hard-bitten pros. First step is to get a list, a long list of likely targets. You then don't do what I am always tempted to do, which is to pick out what looks like the most likely ones.

"Mmm, Mr Savage, don't like the sound of that. Savage by name, savage by nature! Maybe I feel that 9.00 a.m. is a little early to bother people and a nice toddle down to the local cake shop for a doughnut would just move the time along nicely. Wait a moment, though, it is now 10.30 a.m. People will be on their break. Maybe it's time for those doughnuts and a cup of tea. Perhaps, rather than start by ringing potentially hostile strangers, I could ring clients I already have and ones that I know like me – or my mum. Golly, lunchtime already! The end of a tough morning telephone selling.

♩ You must ring every name on that list, one after another.

♩ A script can help but if you just read it you will sound very wooden – but on the other hand, once you have found a form of words that works, stick to them.

♩ Stand up while you make the calls. Firstly, it drops your diaphragm and gives you a better tone and authoritative voice. Secondly, when you are seated, you can relax and fiddle about with distractions. Thirdly, standing up makes it feel so much more like work.

♩ Don't put the receiver down between calls as it breaks concentration and wastes time. You can get into a rhythm by just dipping the receiver with your finger and then going on to the next. One tough guy even suggested taping the receiver to your hand!

I cannot believe I have just recommended the above old-fashioned, unsubtle, pushy technique but the trouble is that it does work. This is the 'numbers game'. Small businesses are failing in their thousands because they don't have enough customers (and by customers I mean profitable customers). These techniques, however coarse, will win you more customers than you need.

The Power of The Phone

Get your foot in the door using the telephone (if you know what I mean).

Ring, ring.

"Acme Tools, Judith speaking."

"Oh hello, Judith. My name is Burch, Geoff Burch."

Explanation

Names are a really tricky subject. In face-to-face conversation the use of the person's name is a key stroke – unless you get it wrong or use it inappropriately. When people ring me on a cold call and call me 'Geoff', I am not happy, but if someone has seen my TV show and calls me 'Geoff', I am happy. It is the same with a client. It must be something to do with status and respect, so if you are in doubt use the most respectful title and ask if this is how they would want to be addressed. The person answering the phone has just given her first name so it is reasonable to assume you have permission to use it. I tend to answer the telephone, "Geoff Burch – how can I help?" If you've got any sense, you will take the safe option by replying, "Oh hello, Mr Burch" because you are unlikely to go wrong. But when making the call, how do I introduce myself? You could try the somewhat sneaky "Tell him it's Geoff..." in the hope that you are mistaken for a chum (fat chance). You could say "Mr Burch" which is a bit naff and will make you look a prat. The best option is surname, followed by first name, followed by surname again. Perhaps you have noticed "The name is Bond...James Bond!" Hard to forget, especially if you have got a white cat and you have been expecting him!

"I wonder if you can help me," then remain silent. People like to help and they also find silence very oppressive. That pressure will then almost always elicit the useful response, "Well, I will try."

You saw Johnny Kaminski do this.

"I wonder if you can tell me who handles purchasing."

"Mr Jackson."

"Is he there?"

Yes, I know it is a closed question but the gatekeeper doesn't want to lie and it sure trumps, "Can I speak to him?"

"Would you put me through to him, please?"

"Can I tell him what it is about?"

Johnny blustered on this one but there are some wrinkles that we can try ironing out. If this is a really important targeted hit, you would have done well to have carried out some research and know the work and the project they are involved in – and how your enterprise could be a part of that.

"I need to speak to him concerning the reconstruction of Paddington Station."

She knows that this is their current biggy and has regularly been putting people through. Perhaps you were fortunate enough to get a lead from a third party (fortune doesn't come into it; I hope you ask every client – actually everyone you meet – if they can recommend useful contacts to you).

"I'm a colleague of Johnny Kaminski and he asked me to contact you."

If it all fails, gobbledygook is often worth a try.

"I wish to discuss his consumption of non-indelible, timber-cladded, graphite covered, calligraphic instruments," (I sell pencils).

She is busy being overwhelmed. In her mind she has done her job, put up the stock obstacles, so puts you through.

Ear to Ear – You Can't Get Face-to-Face on The Telephone

It's a tough fact of life but it is rare to get a major sale or a big decision from that initial phone call. You have just worked hard to get an opportunity to speak to your target person. Don't waste it. Let's rest here for a moment and have a think.

J Tell me, why are you making this call? What do you expect to get from it? An order for a gas-fired power station? The handling of Mega Corp's entire financial affairs?

It is a shame that a book is such a one-way affair. I would love to hear your answers. Remember that we are basing this adventure in persuasion on a journey. Let's look at our map. Sure the final destination is the power station contract but let's look for our first landmark that tells us we are on the way.

Salespeople are sometimes forced to do what in the trade is known as cold calling, which involves appearing unannounced at the target's premises which is even more frightening than doing it on the phone. When I have met these people and asked them what they were doing, the replies were variously, "Trying to sell stuff", "Looking for orders", "Seeing if they wanted anything", "Introducing our company", "Building bridges and forging links!"

What we need in this instance is a simple, clear, and measurable objective. In this case what we want is an appointment – nothing more nothing less.

"Mr Jackson, I am calling you because I would like an appointment to come and see you."

Long silence; you have put your request in, so don't waste it by losing your nerve and gabbling. Silence builds pressure.

A Different Way

This book is here to help you find a different way of doing things, to experience new and challenging flavours in the cookbook of life, so for a bit of fun and nervous excitement try once in a while building embarrassing silences into your everyday conversation (of course not where it will provoke trouble). You will be amazed by the sudden amount of control you achieve and unsolicited information you receive. This is a pressure technique; it is unlikely to make you popular – more interrogator than good listener. Listening skills are the softer side of this – not only will they elicit information but they will make your target love you. However, for now, we have got no time for finesse, the pressure is on!

The silence is broken.

"What about?"

"I'm so glad you asked me that because…"

Can you see the turnaround? It's as if you are responding to his request.

"…I believe I have found a way of saving you a huge amount of money. Would you like to cut costs?"

A question and then silence again.

"Of course. Explain your idea."

"I wish I could but it is impossible on the phone. If I could take just a few moments of your time – do you have your diary to hand?"

Question and wait – but he's not buying yet.

"Look, I'm very busy. Send me details."

"I would love to but I really need to show you the idea. How about next week or would the week after be better for you?"

See here, customers should always have a choice but for Pete's sake don't make one of those choices "No":

"Did you want anything else?"

"Have you had a chance to read my proposal?"

"Did you get my letter?"

"Well, how about it?"

The choice should always be, would you like to do business with me? Or, would you like to do business…with me? "This week or next?"

By the way, if your nerve fails you at this point and you do end up sending details, how do you follow that up:

"Did you receive my email?"

"Did you receive my brochure?"

Oh, how soon they forget! Try not, in these early skirmishes, to ever ask a 'say no' question. Gather up your courage and say,

"Mr Jackson, I emailed some documents through to you and I am now ringing to pick a time that would be convenient for me to come and discuss them with you. How about Tuesday, or would it be better later in the week?"

"Look, you are wasting your time."

"I am so excited about what I am going to show you that I am prepared to invest a few minutes of my time. Will you?"

Every time, a question.

"I haven't got a moment free."

Try a new tack.

"Which is the best hotel in town?"

"Um, the grand Hotel Posh, I think. Why?"

"Well if your diary is full, why don't I treat you to breakfast at the Hotel Posh?"

That was worth a try. Even in the dearest hotel breakfast is often good value and I bet even with a full diary he hasn't got too many 7.30 a.m. appointments.

"No, my office is best. It better not take too long."

"What time do you suggest?"

Here's another oldie but a goodie. Pick a weird time and see what happens.

"How about ten minutes to 10 a.m. or five minutes to 3 p.m.?"

From the above, how long do you think the visit will last? Ten or five minutes? Why? Because I never said anything of the sort – I could be there for hours, but picking times like that gives the impression of precision, punctuality, and a fairly short visit. The other side of this visit is that people in offices are often ruled by diaries, computers or paper that work in fifteen or thirty minute segments. By not picking on the hour, half or even quarter of an hour it is likely to hit a spare moment so you are more likely to be in luck.

POINTS TO PONDER ON CHAPTER 8

1. Forget skill and finesse for a moment - plenty of confidence can carry you through, but a lack of confidence can defeat you.

2. Until your skill becomes a reflex it does no harm at all to work a good script, particularly when using the telephone.

3. Telephone selling is a bit of a myth. What you want are appointments and opportunities that the telephone can grant you. So be very clear and restrict yourself to simply getting that opportunity and don't be tempted to do your full routine on the phone.

4. There is nothing wrong with a nice bit of simplicity. Persistence pays dividends. Even the beggar who goes on and on and on saying "Spare any change" can earn thousands.

CHAPTER 9

NOW YOU'RE ASKING

In which we discover the incredible power of always asking questions

Y ou may feel very uncomfortable with some of the more 'pushy' or 'sales' techniques and worry that it is going right back to the bad old days of insistent obnoxious sales-people. If someone is an expert with the sabre, should they worry about imparting that skill in a book in case people run amok in supermarkets slashing and shouting, "On guard!"? Persuasion, in all its forms, is powerful and should be used responsibly. This bit of pushiness is used just to crack through that shell of resistance to give you the chance to do something wonderful for your customer or friend. When people fail at this they say that it made them uncomfortable, that it is not in their nature to be pushy.

Let's imagine, then, that the world's most magical carnival is coming to your town. You went to it when it came before and you found it an enchanting, enriching and life-changing experience. You cannot wait to go again and this time you want to take your best friend. You phone her and say what?

"Mary, the magic carnival is coming. You have to come!"

"Na, not tonight, I'm washing my hair."

"Don't be silly, you can't miss this. Do your hair another night."

"I'm too tired."

"You're not tired. I'll be round in ten minutes. Be ready!"

Pushy, or what? What's the difference? Oh, it's something you know she would like? You know that she will love it when she gets there? When she sees how marvellous it is, she is going to thank you? Well, dag-nabbit! Just make sure that whatever you offer your customer is going to be just such a thrilling surprise and then you don't need to feel bad, do you?

Actually, this brings us to a very interesting bit of psychology. You may have noticed in the last chapter that I got a bit iffy and fidgety about scripts. There is nothing wrong with a good script that has been proved to work, just so long as the person using it can deliver it with natural convincing enthusiasm. Again, an old chestnut, but that is why in every call centre you will find a sign which says something like, "Smile when you dial". The standing up, the smiling, all help to give you a more convincing tone of voice.

You Only Had to Ask

Now here is a simple persuasion technique that, if you can turn it into a habit, can be literally life-changing. But first, a story. When I speak to a room full of business start-ups and budding entrepreneurs, I pride myself that I can intuitively sort the winners from the duds. As I go around the room, I sort them in my head.

"Terry, what's your idea?"

"Consultancy."

"Doomed!" (Not out loud, of course.)

"Brian?"

"Consultancy."

"Doomed!"

"Steve?"

"A tea shop."

"Don't tell me, you are going to call it The Mad Hatter!"

"How did you guess?"

"Oh, I don't know, just a funny feeling" (and then in my head) "Doomed."

Then I came to a woman who was a cake modeller. She could make and ice cakes in any shape for any occasion. The cakes were brilliant, she was brilliant – what a talent. In that room that day she was the one that I would have picked out to succeed. So imagine my chagrin and surprise when, just a few months later, I found her working at the checkout of our local supermarket.

"What happened to the cake business?" I asked.

"Oh, it was a disaster. I got all them moulds and equipment, then nobody bought them," she replied sadly.

I couldn't understand what had happened. The cakes were wonderful. Why did no one buy them? Then like a bolt from the blue, I realized what she meant. She meant that no one had clambered over the abandoned car in her garden, fought off her savage dog, found her kitchen door, and then asked, "'Ere, you don't make cakes, do you?"

No one bought them – she had never tried to actually get out there and sell them.

When I had received and digested this revelation, I grabbed her arm and hustled her out into the street, doing the Beauty and the Beast thing of 'the first person I see I will persuade'.

Disappointingly, round the corner, came a small, strange, rotund elderly lady, laden down with shopping.

"Do you know anyone who is having a birthday soon?" I asked her.

Her face lit up.

"Oh yes! My little nephew Terry. He's going to be ten! He's a little tinker, into everything – drives his dad mad."

"Ooh, can you imagine what he would make of a cake shaped like a shark, with great big teeth and a diver clamped in its jaws! Blood coloured icing everywhere – oh, and we could make the diver look like his dad!"

"He'd love that. How much are they?"

"Twenty five quid."

"That's a bit much and it ain't his birthday for a couple of weeks."

"Well, it takes a while to make 'em, but look, you only have to give us a fiver deposit and then it'll just be twenty quid – and we deliver it! Go on! You know he'll love it."

Sold to the first person we met.

Just look at your streets, thousands upon thousands of people, all itching to grant you your dearest wish. Maybe not one in one, not even one in ten or one in a hundred, but enough out there to keep you rich and busy forever. The secret? Just ASK! It can change your life. The thing is, we don't ask. In the takeaway, give a big sunny smile to the kid in the paper hat and say, "Give me a few extra fries, please?"

At the Carvery, a smile and a little twitch of the eyebrow, "A bit more meat, please?"

At the theatre, in the cheap seats, "I notice now the show has started, the front stalls are not full. May I move down there please?"

Just see the things you would like and politely ask for them.

"I notice you have a lot of unpicked fruit on your tree. I love apples – do you mind if I harvest them?"

Seriously, what's the worst that can happen? You get told "no". So what. If you always ask at the airline check in desk for a free upgrade, they say no nearly every time, but nearly isn't always, is it? I horribly embarrassed my wife in a very up-market jewellers when I asked for a discount. The poker-straight assistant paused, winced at the word 'discount' but then said, "My manager will allow an adjustment!"

Maybe no discount, but a fifteen percent adjustment felt just as good.

Guided by Vultures

People who know me are usually amazed that I have achieved any level of success and often ask how on earth I did it. Most believe it must have been something that I read.

"What book has guided and inspired you?" they ask. After a great deal of thought I have realized that it is not a book, but a tee-shirt I had when I was a hippy that has guided me to success. On it were two vultures and one vulture is saying to the other, "Patience, my arse! I'm going to go out and kill something!" There is no point sitting on the branch waiting for something to happen. If you want it, then go out there and get it!

IF YOU DON'T ASK, YOU DON'T GET.

The Prizes That Questions Can bring

My hero (or perhaps anti-hero) Machiavelli, said "knowledge is power". Today we are here to get the power to persuade so I suppose it is only logical to say that if knowledge is power, we will need the knowledge to persuade. To continue our journey we need to know if we are talking to the right person. Are they qualified? What is their current situation? What obstacles do they see? What uncertainties and concerns do they have? What secrets do they know about others in their world? How do they see us? What are their dreams for the future?

There is only one way of doing this and that is by asking questions. Questions probably give us more power than any other thing in the pursuit of successful persuasion, and it is something that we will have to come back to time and time again. We can ask for a simple yes or no, or we can create a symphony of clever, carefully planned questions that literally take the person to another place. People tend to underestimate the power of questions and would say that one asks them simply to gain information. So let's take another look.

Questions, of course, give information which is vital, but they also give control, power, and status. It must be part of our early programming but we instinctively respond differently to someone who asks questions. Go back in your mind to your school days. It's a hot summer day, you are feeling tired and distracted, and the boring old History teacher has been droning on and on. "The Hundred Years' War was a reflection of a badly constructed treaty between the advisors of King…" drone, drone, drone, your eyelids droop, your head drops… Then the dynamic of the room suddenly changes. "This brings us on to the incident of Jenkins ear. You! Tell us about Jenkins ear!" You realize that all eyes are on you, he is asking a question, and he is asking you. The room is uncomfortably silent as the pressure builds. That one question has really got your attention.

Try it for yourself, whether you are making a one on one pitch, or presenting to an audience. You may feel you are losing them, they are perhaps bored or perhaps sceptical, but in any event they are fidgety and distracted. What nearly everyone does is get unsettled by the finger tapping, fluff picking, and bogey rolling, and they start to raise the volume or gabble, or – even worse – try to jump their presentation on to something perceived to be more interesting.

"I know, I will tell them the goat, the bishop, and the raspberry jam joke – a bit risqué but should wake 'em up!"

I can hear the whistle of the chill wind and then see the tumbleweed rolling across the back of the room from here. Instead of that, just ask a question. Turn to your listless audience of one, or many, pause for effect and then say, "Look, can I ask you a question?" Then just wait a while. The eyes swing towards you, a little bit more waiting and the pressure will get to them. "Yes, go on," they cry, eager to break the tension. You've got them!

The attention is yours! Are you getting a bit squirmy again? Does it make you feel a bit uncomfortable to think that you can take and hold the attention of a person or a room full of people? In a novel, when a character does something spectacularly unfortunate, someone always says, "And every eye on the room was on her!" Point taken, but without being in control, we aren't going to get anywhere so gird your loins and start using questions to control the structure of your conversations. With that comes a golden bonus for you and that is that these types of question raise your status.

It's a Status Thing

We have been programmed from childhood to accept the status of people who ask us questions. Who asks you questions – the arresting police officers, the judge, your head teacher, or your doctor? Or, more to the point, people from the bottom of the heap tend to ask fewer questions. OK, the waiter or the dimwitted shop assistant will ask one stock, kick-off question, "Are you ready to order?", "Can I help you?"

But usually this is a cue for either you to give them orders or to interrogate them. "I'll have steak and chips, please." "Are the meat balls edible?" "Do you sell light bulbs?"

Their status can be raised if they can answer your question with a question:

"The meat balls, sir – well, do you enjoy the flavour of game?"

"Where in your home will you be using these light bulbs?"

Look in your head right now at the person pictured in the above. At the "Do you sell light bulbs?" stage, you pictured a bottom-scratching kid with vacant eyes, but at the "Where in your home will you be using…" bit, that person has matured and grown in stature, to perhaps someone you wouldn't want to intimidate. That is the power of questions.

I try to do it all the time. Someone said to me recently, "Geoff, why do you always answer a question with a question?" My reply, "Do I?"

Questions GIVE YOU STATUS!

Games People Play

One of my favourite books is *Games People Play* by the eminent psychologist Eric Berne. It appeals to my dark sense of humour as Berne sets down, using the science of transactional analysis, how every dysfunctional and destructive behaviour is actually a game that has players, rules, winners and losers. Games such as 'Alcoholic', and 'Now look what you made me do'. My favourite is one called 'Yes, but…'. The game, as I understand it, is for the key player to have a terrible problem which they take to a friend, colleague or partner. The victim is enticed into offering solutions. She appears weeping,

"My husband beats me."

You reply, "You poor thing. Leave him."

"Yes, but I love him." Now it starts.

"Well, tell him how you feel."

"Yes, but he never listens."

"Then you should go and seek professional help."

"Yes, but it's him that needs the help."

"Well, threaten to leave him."

"Yes, but that's why he beat me up in the first place."

"Well I don't know what to suggest – it's got me beat."

It didn't beat you, she did! You may even detect a little smirk of victory if you look closely. My dad, the psychiatrist, had patients like that but he understood the game and had a counter game.

"My husband beats me!"

"You poor thing. I am so sorry to hear that, and what are you planning to do about it?"

"Um, well, I could leave him."

"But don't you love him?"

The power of questions again. The people we try to persuade will all play that game with us in one form or another.

At the job interview, "…yes, but don't you feel you are a bit young for this position?"

The sales pitch, "…yes, but how do you see this being better than our current supplier?"

The lovers, "Yes, but I wouldn't wish to commit to just one person for the rest of my life!"

TRY

"So after reading my CV, why do you feel I could be the right candidate for this post?"

"Where do you feel we need to improve on your current supplier?"

"What attracted you to me in the first place?"

Ask The Way

Our map analogy drops to bits a little here but the journey thing doesn't. Let me explain. We have, together, developed this idea that persuading someone from one place to another is like some kind of journey. In any such adventure, we clearly need to know where we are, where we were, and where we are going. If we have a map, we can use our eyes to tell us where we are, but without a map the only answer is to ask when we get lost! If you are a Granny, you may feel that there is a bit of 'egg sucking' advice coming on, but here goes.

"What's the name of this town?"

"How far is it to the next village?"

"Is there a petrol station near here?"

It seems obvious, and it's something we all do with little discomfort. So why on earth don't we do it in conversation with people from whom we want something important?

We can clearly see that a conversation constructed with a high proportion of questions from our side gives more attention, more status, and more information. But what information is it that we want?

Imagine your devastating telephone technique has got you that all-important appointment, and before you go to it, you and I sit down for a nice chat to discuss the visit.

Q. Why are you going to see this person?

A. To tell him a bit about my offer, to demonstrate my product.

Then think about this. What problem does he have that your product can solve? Can your demonstration show the solution they are looking for? Who is their current supplier? How are they currently solving this problem? Are you talking to the right person? This is just a fraction of the things you need to find out, but let's start with a rather important one – are you talking to the right person? You will remember how vital it was that you appeared qualified to be permitted to persuade the other person, but just as important is, are they qualified to give you what you want?

A Night of Passion with Chummy

When I was young, not far from my home town was a west country city with a thriving dock area (everyone sounded like a Hollywood pirate), which meant that seamen from all over the world were searching the streets at night for fun and frolics. There was a very flamboyant transvestite who the locals called Chummy. The sailors would spend time and money flattering Chummy and plying him with drinks because he appeared to be a seductive leggy blonde – with whom they hoped to have their wicked way! When finally, while enveloped in a loving clinch, they discovered the surprising truth, they tended to chuck Chummy in the dock. It was quite a regular occurrence for the police to come in the early hours of the morning and fish Chummy out of the oily water. A few simple qualifying questions could have avoided all this unpleasantness!

If you read any of the traditional sales training books, they make a huge fandango about this qualifying thing, and they are not entirely wrong – but where they are wrong is that they suggest if the object of your persuasion fails the qualification process you should walk away. As you will see, everyone has something useful to offer on our journey.

Shallow

Recently, I have been heavily involved with the world of television. As a relatively new boy, I had never encountered a world like it before – I think the expression 'shallower than a puddle' would be an injustice to the profundity of puddles. We were at a dinner party of the glitterati and proto-glitterati, where I was disturbed to see my wife clearly being chatted up by some slick and perfumed Lothario. They to'd and fro'd banter for a while until what I took to be a witty put-down from my missus caused him to turn his back on her and talk to someone else for the rest of the evening.

"Wow," I said, "what did you do?"

She said, "When he discovered I wouldn't sleep with him and I couldn't give him his own quiz show, he lost interest!" Not qualified, then! Where he lost out on this occasion was that he missed the unspoken cliché, "but I know a man who can!" (The quiz show, not the bed part... .) The truth is that everyone can give us useful direction on this journey. When we get lost, we stop and ask someone the way. If you were being a bit bumptious you could say that the person's ability to direct us may depend on their status and position in the world.

Ask a Local

If we were travelling to Anchorage, Alaska, and got a bit disorientated in the village of Nether Wapping, would this mean that the ancient rustic sitting on a gate could not give any helpful direction because he had no knowledge of the American arctic regions? What he has got is an encyclopedic knowledge of Nether Wapping and its surrounding area. How far his knowledge stretches is for us to find out with careful and delicate qualifying questions. What we are doing, unlike our vapid diner, is qualifying people to be of assistance, not to dismiss them as useless.

POINTS TO PONDER ON CHAPTER 9

1. It doesn't feel pushy if you are offering something that you know they would love.

2. Being warm and friendly is a strong persuasive tool.

3. Are there things you would like to have? Then simply go out and ask for them.

4. Questions give you the power to get attention.

5. Questions give you status.

6. Questions give you information.

7. Of course you have to be qualified, but is the person you are persuading qualified to give you what you want?

8. It is often said that you should make sure you are talking to the right person, but everybody is the right person as everyone has something to give that is helpful. It is only by using careful questioning that we can find out what that thing is.

CHAPTER 10

THE CUNNING PLAN

In which we start to pull the threads together
by planning who, where, when, why, and how

Whilst just a callow youth, I gravitated towards sales jobs because in my mind they were an easy option. My performance was chaotic, but instinctive, so I tended to produce enough figures to stay in work. Pause here for some festery old motivational sayings:

"He didn't plan to fail, he failed to plan!"

Or:

"Don't plan to work, work to plan!"

Neither of the above meant a thing to me until I encountered a grizzled old sales manager who realized I was getting along by flying courtesy of the seat of my pants. He gave me a scrap of paper and said, "Every time you leave a call, answer these questions or you're fired!" I had the plan now and would have to work it. As I am a scatological mess, this little bit of paper changed everything for me and it may help you. It had on it a few simple questions:

1. **Did I achieve my chosen goal for this visit?** I know that the threat is that I will be fired if I don't answer the questions when I leave the call but if I hadn't got a goal when I went in I could hardly answer in the affirmative when I

come out. If you are going to visit someone on a mission of persuasion, then have a very clear idea exactly what it is that you want to achieve. It doesn't even matter if you don't achieve what you set out to do – as long as you have set down what your objective is you can at least judge where you are in relation to it.

In quantum mechanics there is a puzzle called Schrödinger's Cat which rambles on a bit about isotobes and half life, but the fun bit is that you lock a cat in a box with a potentially lethal bit of nuclear doings. Now, without opening the box, tell me, is the cat dead or alive? See – you can't be sure, so the dotty professors, to fiddle their results and convince us that the planet grew from a cosmic stone or something, say that the cat is in a state which is both alive and dead – or neither alive nor dead. This is, of course, cobblers, but while we give a little chuckle we must face the fact that this is how we tend to live our lives. That lottery ticket in your pocket is the winner until you see the results. That scratch card has as good a chance as any until we scratch it. Don't look under rocks, don't look under your teenager's bed, don't look at the timbers in the loft, and all will be well with the world. That's why 'v.int' is so comforting, because as long as we can keep that going we don't have to hear a big fat 'no'. It's time for a change. Before you go in, choose and decide a clear goal and then ask clear questions about the progress you are making.

2. **What am I learning about this person, this company, this situation?** This is the next item on this checklist. Even if you have been saddled with the office boy don't write the visit off. Just ask those valuable questions, for example, "So who is in charge of this project?", "I notice an office is being redecorated. Is someone getting a promotion?", "What is your company planning to do in that new

extension?" Those little nuggets can often be pure gold. A few days later, Derek Pile receives a letter from you congratulating him on becoming a partner and offering him a celebratory lunch. Something else requires mentioning here – which is, whoever you meet, treat them with respect and deference. That dozy kid may well be the managing partner's son, the funny old chap on the bicycle you shout abuse at on the way in, is the managing partner. Always bear that in mind – everyone you meet is important.

3. **Ask the person you are with what they know about their world in general.** "I see the office block next door has been finally let. Who is moving in there?", "Who else in your field is involved in this process?" In a professional environment I tend to write everything down. This may, or may not, seem obvious but it is actually very rare. We somehow believe that reading and writing make us look incompetent or inattentive when actually the reverse is true. I have a bit of an issue with people who smoke pipes. When you address them they start this tapping, scratching, lighting, and puffing thing which seems to orchestrate the conversation to their choice of timing. That has the result of enraging me because I feel it is a sort of bullying, but in a much more gentle and subtle way writing things down can give that same control without the irritation. "They are doing what? Wow! Let me just make a note of that. Can you spell that for me, please?" That note-taking alters the pace, shows genuine interest, and will be so useful later.

4. **If you got every outcome you planned for and if you repeated that meeting, what would you do to improve your performance?** This is the final question you need to ask yourself. There is always something and this means that you just get better and better at persuading.

A Drama in Three Acts

As we penetrate the obstacles and the people who stand in our way to our goal of meeting the decision maker, we may have to accept that the decision maker might not make the decision. Before you decide that this could be more confusing than Schrödinger's Cat, consider this situation.

You represent a company which makes a machine that revolutionizes the manufacture of table legs. Your machine is not cheap but in a couple of years of accelerated leg-spinning, the initial investment will be handsomely repaid. You must be confident that this should be an easy sell and, even better, you have got an appointment with Sir Gordon Hepplewite-Castor-Drawleaf of Castor Drawleaf tables. Sir Gordon's flabber is completely ghasted! He is won over. "Blow the money," he cries, "I love it. I want it. I shall have it!" Job done then? Not a bit of it. Let's examine the cast list of this three act tragedy and then we may understand.

Players

Sir Gordon Hepplewite-Castor-Drawleaf – el supremo of Castor Drawleaf
Terry Dismal – Finance Director and depressive
Brian Put-on – Factory manager
Sid Downs – Machinist
The Sinister Spy

Sir Gordon is, without doubt, the lord of all he surveys, but to him you are not the most important person in his life. In truth, you are one of the least. He wants the machine because it amused and entertained him for a moment. He likes new toys but he hates hassle and confrontation. He also is not over-interested in commercial implications – he has more money than he can spend and if he shut the company down, moved production to China and sold the acres of industrial land he owns, he would have many millions. So, in his own mind he keeps the place open as a sort of charity. Through his office door steams Mr Dismal, the finance director. "Sir Gordon, we have been passed this order for this Leggomat Five Thousand. That is a huge amount of money and it is not in this year's budget. What is the justification?"

Sir Gordon cannot remember the justification, he just liked the whirly cogwheels and coloured lights.

This is where Put-on appears. "What is all this about a new machine? Where am I supposed to put that and who will train the operator? There aren't enough hours in the day!"

Meanwhile, there is a hubbub of noise from outside as Sid Downs and his fellow union brothers come out on strike to protest at the mechanization taking honest, working men's jobs.

Your careful investigation where you took notes should have revealed this potential for trouble. Each person will have to be persuaded separately with convincing arguments tailored for each of them, and then perhaps together. The finance guy will probably value a presentation that involves facts and figures which show increased profits and honour and reward for him. The factory manager can see how your free machinery-installation planning service will make him a star – and when Sid stays at a rather nice hotel near your works to have hands-on training, he will see that he can do less work and double his bonus.

The spy? He is yours! It may seem a bit cloak and dagger to suggest that you hang around in bars trying to corrupt the unwary but literally seeing a guy in overalls and buying him a drink can reveal secrets you would never normally know.

"Oh, I see you work opposite! Isn't that the place owned by Sir Gordon, that bloke off the telly? Does he have much to do with the day-to-day running of the place?"

"Nah. The real gaffer is the miserable git from finance, Terry Dismal. If it wasn't for his passion for toy soldiers I don't think we would believe he was even human."

I'm not going to suggest what you could do with a conversation like that because I bet you are one step ahead of me.

The key to this whole thing is understanding the influence all the players have on events. You have sometimes no idea of the off-stage conversations and you will have to gather evidence and clues to make a good shot at calculating what is going on. It happens in virtually every persuasion project we get involved in. There are some fabulous books on high level negotiating, advanced selling, and personal relationships, but they often fail to take into account the influence of the unseen or neglected characters. If you sell cars, you have the husband and wife come in. She stands meekly by while he views the executive saloon. He addresses pertinent technical questions to you, to which you reply to the best of your ability. What you didn't see is the conversation that preceded their visit. "Henry Warton. You are not having a new car; you know we can't afford it. I will tolerate half an hour in that showroom but don't you dare agree to anything. Do you understand?"

"Yes dear."

What you hear when addressing her is, "My husband makes all the decisions."

We can sometimes use knowledge of psychology and body language to identify the real movers and shakers, but to be safe try and spot everyone involved and convince them all.

POINTS TO PONDER ON CHAPTER 10

1. It doesn't matter how naturally clever you are at persuading, you can always improve results by having a clear plan.

2. Determine exactly what you want before you start the process.

3. Even if you don't achieve what you set out to, always make sure that you come away with plenty of useful information that you can use on another occasion.

4. The old cliché of the decision-maker can be very misleading and there are often a lot of people that you don't even see that are involved in the decision.

5. Don't be afraid to recruit a spy for that useful inside information.

CHAPTER 11

A.I.D.A.
OLD BUT STILL LOVELY

In which we learn about A.I.D.A., the classic
sales formula that can still be used in every
aspect of modern persuasion

One of the ancient formulas will give us a good skeleton
on which to flesh out the idea of the structured sale.
The one I have in mind is A.I.D.A. This acronym stands
for Attention, Interest, Desire, and Action. It isn't the whole
picture, in fact there is a very large piece of the puzzle missing, but for now let's just examine A.I.D.A.'s logic.

Pay Attention

Pay attention to persuade someone you really need their
attention. In the early days of door-to-door selling it was
soon realized that knocking on someone's door and saying
something like, "Do you need a vacuum cleaner?" meant
that the potential purchaser lost their attention very quickly
indeed. It is a simple fact that no persuasion – or in fact
any communication – can take place unless you have the
other person's attention. What really frustrates me as a

professional communicator of persuasion techniques is all the professionals who start the 'we've done that!', "Poo, not rotten old A.I.D.A. again!" or, if they are being charitable, "Well, it's always important to be reminded of what you already know." When coaching one-to-one I then see the whole thing fly out of the window. In a written test they can quote A.I.D.A. chapter and verse yet they fall at the first hurdle. Do they have the other person's full attention? How often, when on the telephone, do you notice a sort of vagueness that you can't quite put your finger on? Then you hear the clickety clack of the keyboard or the Microsoft jingle...yep, they are doing their emails. Talking at people is a sure way of losing their attention but we do need to get our point across.

Child's Play

When considering the mechanics of persuasion I did wonder why such a cheesy old acronym as A.I.D.A. was so important and why even the most elevated of persuaders found such a simple old technique so difficult to stick to. Let us examine our map analogy again. With every journey there has to be stages which physically cannot be taken out of order. Where our persuasion journey comes to bits is that it can be taken out of order with fairly disastrous results.

Kids are the greatest persuaders I have ever seen. They lack the sophistication of adult guile so they make the fundamental error of asking for their goal and then trying to post-justify it if turned down. This can work but it takes the brass neck of a child to pull it off. In my book *Resistance is Useless*, I suggested a six-year-old child can do a better job of persuasion than us.

"Dad, can I have a lolly?" This is not A.I.D.A. Attention is not guaranteed. But what am I saying? The kid knows by instinct so a lot of sleeve-tugging and "Dad, Dad, Dad, Dad..." will take place until there is indeed attention.

Dad, "No."

Child, "Why not?" Questions sell better than statements.
Dad, "You won't eat your tea."
Child, "If I promise to eat my tea then can I have a lolly?"
A classic negotiating statement and yet another question.
Dad, still wriggling, "No."
"Why not?" Do you still have the nerve to do this? You used to!
"Your Mum would kill me!"
"Mummy doesn't have to know." A valuable conspiratorial concession. Dad is lost but doesn't know it yet.
"OK, you can have a fruity one."
"I want a chocolate one!" When you have crushed all opposition, go for everything you can get.
If you just copied the kid your chances of persuasion would improve – try it, if you dare.
"Mr Smith, can I have your cleaning contract, please?"
"No!"
"Why not?"
"Because I don't know you from Adam."
"If we could demonstrate our success with companies like yours, could we have your cleaning contract?"
"No."
"Why not?"
"Your prices are too high."
"If we could show that our service could save you money and make you money, can we have your contract?"
"Maybe I could try you in this building."
"If you give us the whole complex you could save even more!"

Any Outcome, a Happy One

This is a crude fantasy that even I might be a little shy of using. But ask yourself, how far is that from your current interaction with potential customers? There is of course a 'but', and it is a whacking great big 'but', and that is that the kid's persuasion technique is instinctive shoot-from-the-hip stuff that lacks any kind of structure. Strangely, that is also how kids travel – they hurtle about, perhaps pedalling furiously on their bicycles expending joyous energy on their travels. If they know where they are going they go there, if they are not sure they crash about until they get where they want to be, or until they arrive somewhere unexpected but more interesting than where they thought they were going. The lolly persuader would have accepted a hot dog or, weirdly enough, a fairground ride as a satisfactory outcome for the lolly request. As grown-ups our persuasion must be more targeted and structured. There is not much point seeing our potential clients about a new contract and coming away with a dart board. A kid would be happy with that (The truth is so would I! It drives my wife/boss nuts. "How was your meeting with the publisher? Have you negotiated the Australian rights?" "No, but better than that, I bought his motorbike!")

They Knew What They were Doing

The word is *structure*. A.I.D.A. does one very special thing and that is it creates a structured interaction. This is the key element that turns the normal conversation or interaction into the persuasive one. This demands a surprisingly large amount of mental application and concentration. In other words, the whole interaction is planned and intentional, and during the whole process you will – or should be – acutely aware of where you are. I doubt that anyone could keep that up for long and I am sure that the professional persuaders often step outside their body and coldly and calculatingly observe themselves and their opposition, judging exactly where they are in the process. There are ever more sophisticated process diagrams but if we don't operate something as easy as A.I.D.A. consciously, how on earth could we master something more complicated?

Let's get back to our vacuum salesperson. Instead of, "Do you want a new vacuum?", he will try an attention grabber. Nothing dramatic but a simple, "Good morning! Do you own a vacuum cleaner?"

Sounds daft but a question like that grabs your attention and sets you up for the next bit, whether "No" or "Yes".

"No" of course means you are ripe for the demonstration of this miraculous labour-saving device.

"Yes" gets a "but can it do this?"

Knockers

The classic on-the-knocker salesperson would always try to contrive an opportunity for a tricksy, even spectacular demonstration of the machine's stunning abilities (yep, the dem!). They would suddenly leap forward and tip soot on your white carpet, only for your horror to be replaced by amazement when not only would the soot be sucked away without a trace, but that the patch of carpet came up cleaner than the surrounding one. They would tell you how clearly house-proud you were and how immaculate your house was. You couldn't possibly have it cleaner, could you? They would vacuum your spotless floor and then to your horror they would empty the bag with piles of un-noticed foulness that your current machine had betrayed you by missing. Or, they would use their device's enormous power to stick it to your ceiling, all of which secures your INTEREST.

Objects of Desire

But do you want such a machine? Now you must DESIRE it.

The desire stage is a fascinating one because it relates to the prospect's specific, "what's in it for me" situation. This is where the old school and I again part company. In the classic A.I.D.A. vacuum- selling situation, the salesperson should deduce what is important specifically to the prospect so that desire can be created. I agree that it would be nice to do that, but unless you are psychic it can be a bit tricky. The truth is that this component of the persuasion process which relates precisely to the other person's exact situation is one of the key components, and the old timers realized this and dealt with it with more acronyms – one of which is F.B.I.

I can hear another huge groan from the professionals out there. F.B.I is as old as the hills, all the pros know it, and the world has moved on. It may be a sound truth but surely we all know it. Yet as you watch the best professional presentations, dear old F.B.I. is ignored. First let me explain how it works.

FBI Agent

'F' stands for feature. Examples are, 'This car has a big engine; this soup is tinned; this company has twenty offices' – things that are often stated by us when we are trying to describe ourselves, our company, or our product. Look at your CV. Look at the opening slide of your PowerPoint presentation, or the first page of the company report. To be kind, I suppose we could describe your offering as feature-rich. From your prospect you get a big fat "So what?"

A bore is someone who talks about themselves when you want to talk about yourself! We need to see what's in it for them, how they can 'B' for benefit. If you want to find the benefit there is a very simple exercise you can use, and that is with every fact you state, add the phrase "which means that". For example, "This soup is tinned, which means that it has an almost limitless shelf life." "This car has a big engine, which means that it goes like the clappers!" "This company has twenty offices which means that every town in the county is covered." That should have got it sorted then, but to our surprise all that elicits is another "So what?". What we need is to find the incentive that makes them relate all this to their own lives.

'I' is for incentive and we find that by adding, "And that means you can..."

"This soup is tinned, which means that it has an almost limitless shelf life, and that means you can go to the cupboard and have a delicious nutritious bowl of soup at any time!"

"This car has a big engine which means that it goes like the clappers, and that means you can be admired by your friends for your speed and daring!"

"This company has twenty offices which means that every town in the county is covered, and that means you can be sure help is never far away."

It's Easy to Assume

Now this is very simple and unsophisticated and it is tradi-tional at this point to show how benefits and incentives are useless if they don't relate specifically to the other person's precise circumstances. There is, in actual fact, a very irri-tating reminder of this that states: 'ASSUME makes an ASS of U and ME'. Ho, ho! So witty. Of course, the more precise we can be the better, and we penetrate the mists of investigation elsewhere in this book but the truth is you aren't stupid and a bit of assumption isn't that bad. If the person you are talking to admits to being a getaway driver for a team of bank robbers, I think it would be reasonable to assume we know why a fast car might be desirable. Just for now, bear in mind F.B.I. whenever you state facts and features about what point you are trying to put across.

If you think this is old hat, next time you are plunged into darkness with your colleagues at the conference and the guest speaker pulls up his opening slide with a huge list of what his company is doing, you will spot lots of 'F's' and no 'B's' or 'T's'. At this your eyelids will flicker and blessed sleep saves you from an hour of bum-numbing tedium. Before you drifted away, did it say things like, "The world's largest manufacturer of cat food", "A major player in 40 countries", "An enviable employees' welfare package". Are you perhaps feeling a touch uncomfortable at this point? Is it because this is how your presentation looks? Is this how your conversations look? I know I am banging on about this simple thing but the truth is that even though it is simple it is difficult to remember to apply the "what's in it for them" thinking to every statement you make. "I've got a black belt in karate, which means that I can defend myself – and that means you can be safe walking home with me!"

The real persuasion, of course, takes place in the sweaty face-to-face furnace of one-to-one interaction where investigative questioning can give you killer precision. But for a lot of persuasive situations we have to assume or guess our prospect's hot buttons, when we chat up strangers, when we advertise, when we present, or when we write copy. With this book I have to guess what parts of the persuasive process will entertain and even delight you. If we met and you told me about your persuasive desires I could custom-build the programme for you – which means you could persuade exactly the people you wanted to, and that means you can expect to become a lot richer (of course I have to make a wild guess at you wanting to be richer).

So there it is, F.B.I. Simple or not, work it for all its worth. This is what creates the DESIRE in A.I.D.A.

Action Plan

The final 'A' is **ACTION**. The salespeople of old were obsessed with this one and on a most basic level they called it "closing the sale". There were international road shows attracting thousands of people that were simply about closing the sale, books were written by the hundreds on closing the sale and, as I have already said, sales jobs were advertised as simply "Good closers wanted!" Of course, all this was a bit misguided because a lot of intelligent work needs to be done before the other person is convinced enough to give a positive decision, but where they were right was in spotting people's lack of skill and reluctance to actually ask for a decision.

Imagine you have been chatting cheerfully to a customer. Let's strip away all manners, all subtlety and technique and simply say, "Well, are you going to buy it then?" What's going to happen? Will you be attacked, vilified or humiliated? Probably the very worse thing that could happen is that the other person says "no". The whole early sales business was dedicated to making that answer "yes".

The number one answer we want is "yes" but second place goes to "no" because there are far worse answers than "no". For example, "I'm very interested, but…", "I'd like to think it over..." or, worst of all, no tangible conclusive answer because you didn't actually ask them to buy anything. So for this part of our journey and without any special skills or subtlety you can improve your situation enormously by simply asking for some ACTION.

Get "No" and I'll Pay You

I often recount a story of a commission-only sales company that paid 100 dollars for every sale made but discovered that their salespeople's cold call hit rate was about three percent – or in other words, out of one hundred complete strangers that they jumped out on, three would buy. If you wanted to double your wages, jump out on two hundred people. Direct sell salespeople call that the 'numbers game'. Then the company got a new owner who changed the commission structure. For every signed up 'yes' they still paid 100 dollars, but for a signed up 'no' they paid 10 dollars. For you mathematicians out there this may suggest that if sales ran at current levels the potential earnings should have been 300 dollars for the 'yes' result and 970 dollars for the 'no', but what actually happened was the 'no's were nearly as hard to get as the 'yes's.

"So, Madam, that is my demonstration concluded. If you could just OK the agreement, I can proceed."

(By the way, 'OK'ing the agreement' is a lot more persuasive than 'signing the contract' but that is a complication we can live without at the moment.)

"Well, I'm not sure; I really need to think about it."

"Well, Madam, this other agreement says, 'I hate your product, I will never buy it, and all I agree to is a big fat NO! Could you OK this?"

"Does that mean I could never buy one?"

"Well, I suppose it does."

"I'd have to think about that. I'd never like to just say no!"

What happens is that the yes's increase to about ten. What the new structure had done was provoke the sales team to force a decision one way or the other. Once again the lesson is, don't be afraid to ask. Persuasion really kicks in and starts at 'no'. It gets a bit stuck at 'I'll think about it',or, worse, silence.

Of course our pioneer chum clearly would like to improve the chances of getting a 'yes'. This comes down to picking the correct moment. Firstly, if you had successfully completed the path set down by one of your acronyms (in our case, A.I.D.A.), if in stage three we have caused a dribbling, panting, uncontrolled desire in our subject, then proposing the ACTION that would let them process the object of their desire should be a mere formality. It rarely is, of course, and spotting the drool moment isn't always that easy.

POINTS TO PONDER ON CHAPTER 11

1. Have you got the other person's full attention? Check this out because without it there is no point in continuing.

2. Whilst you are at it, are they really interested (no, not 'very interested')?

3. Simple questions can build desire.

4. For heaven's sake, ask them to buy something.

5. If you want to see one of the best persuaders in the world, ask a child.

6. Even if the answer is "no" it is better than "maybe" or no answer at all.

CHAPTER 12

SHOWBUSINESS

In which we discover the surrounding magic
that makes our core skills attractive

Before we move forward, this putting on a show thing is
worthy of further comment. The fact is that most of us
don't (put on a show, that is)! We get obsessed by what we
do, and we think that just because what we do, sell, or make
is good or even the best, people will be obliged to buy it.

When I speak to my business start-ups, they all list their
skills, talents, and products, but that is not what we humans
buy. We buy the package, the experience. Think about this.
Disneyland is a funfair where machines whirl you about in
an attempt to make you chuck. If a funfair arrives at your
town, you pay a pound or so for a ride and don't feel that it
is any kind of great bargain. Yet with the cost of flights, we
pay hundreds or even thousands of pounds for Disneyland.
People believe it heals sick children ("Tammy is ill. £3000
could send her to Lourdes but if we could raise £5000 it
could be Disneyland".) So what's different? "People dressed
as cartoon characters," you cry. Every amusement park in the
world has tried that one but it doesn't make them Disney. It
is all about how they do it and the surrounding magic.

A Proper Hairdresser

I often tell the story of a woman on one of our courses who was, without doubt, one of the best hairdressers that anyone had ever seen. Due to family commitments she had left her city salon job and decided to start up on her own. She would tell anyone who asked that her business was hairdressing. She had a small van and offered a mobile service. One week one of her regular ladies said, "Don't come next month, dear, come the month after." When she did come, the customer's hair looked a terrible mess.

"What happened to you?" she cried.

"Oh, it was my boy's wedding, so I went to a proper hairdresser!"

I don't have a hair salon but if I did and you visited Salon Geoff, I would pay as much attention to the Café Latte, the smoked salmon sarnies, the best magazines and fresh flowers, and would tell you that you had come to be made beautiful!

Astonishingly, few businesses acknowledge the value of the 'show' – which is a big element of persuasion.

Come on Baby, Light My Fire

In the money tree story in Chapter 3, we discovered that a sulphurous demon rising in a pillar of fire was quite persuasive. On a little more down to earth level, if you eat a crepe on a blind tasting, you may not differentiate one pancake-type product from another, but when a flunkey dressed like a penguin arrives at your table pushing a silver trolley and with a flourish sets fire to the thing, all of a sudden a huge amount of value is added. Before going forth to persuade, be sure that you are putting on the very best show possible. Your appearance, the product's appearance, the time and the place must all be concomitant with the message you are trying to deliver.

Some airlines have hip and trendy teams that, in actual fact, grate on me so much I won't fly with them, but that doesn't matter as I am not their target customer (it is the formal stuffy and stiffer type of airlines that makes me feel safe). Clearly you must plan your show to precisely fit your audience. An awful lot of time is wasted persuading or trying to impress the wrong people. Know your audience, your subject, or your customer, and then tailor your presentation to your interpretation of what you feel they would enjoy. You are not going to appeal to everybody, and if you try to it can fatally dilute your energy.

This thought that all persuasion leads to the solution of a problem throws up a few more problems of our own.

Rock and Roll

In the section on F.B.I. (Chapter 11), the concept of benefits is discussed. To remind you: the idea that the features of what we offer mean nothing to our subject until they are converted into the "What's in it for me" benefits, or even better, further turned into the "and that means you can…" incentives. But the sales trainers then try to sell us a fiction. This is, in its most simple form, illustrated as a see-saw. Imagine our subject at the far end of a see-saw, weighed down with a box of rocks. These rocks are their inertia, prejudices, and problems. Say the subject has three rocks of "It's too dear", "We are quite happy with the people we use", and "I don't like the colour", if you can produce four or more yummy rocks of benefits at your end of the see-saw, things must surely tip your way. But what convention doesn't allow for is the size of the rock. "Setting aside the fact that this wedding dress is scarlet, you can afford it, and I am sure you will agree that the cut makes you look slimmer." In this case, the "I don't like the colour" rock is so huge that the benefits rocks will never outweigh it.

Apart from That, Mrs Lincoln, How was The Play?

Some of the most sophisticated commercial persuasion systems still persist with this see-saw model. They describe the customer's end as weighted down with the fuss, bother, and cost of a change, whilst their offering – using features, benefits, incentives, and demonstration – creates, in their words, a "value proposition" that outweighs all of this. I don't wholly disagree with this; a stark example would be your central heating packs up in mid-winter and the plumber leads you to realize that your decorations will be wrecked, the house will be cold and full of workmen for a week, and it will cost five grand! That is the best value on offer and you go for it, but it will leave you feeling a bit sore. The problem with problem solving is that people who have problems tend not to be happy; even when the problem is solved, if the solution is painful they may be relieved but not actually happy. The man trapped under a rock by his foot in a rising tide hacks the offending limb off with a penknife. Problem solved? Yes. Happy? I doubt it.

Take a Load off Me

So picture the scene. The subject is at the far end of the see-saw, weighed down with this huge pile of prejudices, dissatisfactions and concerns. We load our end with the benefits or even value of what we offer until his end rises from the ground. To progress this somewhat tenuous analogy a bit further, I suppose you could say that the physical construction of the see-saw is in fact the relationship between us and the subject. If they have a huge load on their end and we try to out-balance them by piling on stuff at our end, the see-saw will come under huge tension. Picture it curved nearly to breaking point with the subject rising and falling accompanied by an alarming sound of cracking. Whilst that plumber was the only one to come out over Christmas, they made you pay dearly for it and you will never love them for it. Piling on the benefits is a sort of pressure.

Let The Sunshine in

In every book I have ever written, I am sure I mention Aesop's fable of the sun and the wind. This will be no exception because it is at the heart of what I believe to be the best route to persuasion. If you don't know it, the story goes that the sun and the wind were bowling around the Heavens having an argument as to who was the most powerful. They saw an unsuspecting human far below wearing a thick coat. "I bet I can get that coat off him," the wind declared. "You're on," said the sun, "a tenner says you can't!" The wind gathered all its force and, howling down from the sky, it hit the man at full power. He ended up tumbling down the road like an autumn leaf but with every blast he pulled the coat tighter and tighter around him. In the end the wind gave up exhausted.

"OK," he admitted to the sun, "you win. That guy will never let that coat go."

"I can get it," grinned the sun. "Want to get your money back double or quits?"

"You're on."

The sun rose majestically into the sky where he smiled and shone and blazed. The flowers opened, the puddles dried, the birds began to sing. The man mopped his sweating brow, smiled, and of course took his coat off (while singing, I am sure, Zippidy doo dah!). Will your customers be singing zippidy doo dah once you have finished with them?

Selling a Negative

Rather than pile the pressure on our end of the see-saw, we would do better to lighten the load at the other end. We do that by discovering the concerns with gentle questioning, acknowledging their importance, sympathizing with the consequences, and then removing them by agreement. Every guru worth their salt has to have a three-letter acronym and I am no exception. I have created P.N.C which stands for Problem, Negafit, and Consequence. It works like F.B.I. only backwards. Instead of us stating a feature of our offer which leads to a benefit which leads to an incentive, in the same way that the subject doesn't naturally see benefits when features are mentioned, they don't always see the ramifications of their problem.

Problem statement: "I have my foot trapped under this rock."

Our solution: "We can soon get you out."

Customer's concern: "How? I've been trying for ages."

Our solution: "May have to cut your foot off."

Let's try P.N.C.

Problem statement: "I have my foot trapped under this rock."

Negafit statement: "Which means that you won't be moving far from here any time soon."

Consequences statement: "And that means that with this rising tide you could be in trouble."

People have to acknowledge the cost of the problem before they can appreciate the value of the solution. Putting on a show is perhaps a slightly shallow way of describing how, through professionalism, understanding, and perfect timing, we can encourage our subject to increase the value in their mind of what we are offering. Perhaps more importantly, if we don't take into consideration the surrounding magic that our professionalism can produce, we can actually devalue or negate the value of our proposition.

It's Nice to be Nice

I realize this sounds a bit soppy after all this tough stuff but always make an effort to be nice. If that plumber appeared with a huge bunch of flowers just to say sorry for the disruption, to thank you for being one of the nicest customers they'd ever had, and to assure you that you have invested in the finest and most prestigious example of home heating, you would feel a lot happier about the situation. The old sales adage that you only cry once when you buy quality does mean that you do need to convince the other party that they have made a good decision. I tell every retail salesperson that when they have made a sale they should compliment and congratulate the customer on their purchase. If you think this is a bit touchy-feely, the truth is that almost every decision or purchase we make is driven by our emotions. Ignore this at your peril or understand and control it to your eternal benefit. This is so important that later we devote a section to the psychology of persuasion, but for now, back to our persuading through problem solving.

Oh, Doctor, I'm in Trouble

A really interesting interaction that I often use as an example is the relationship between a doctor and a patient. The more deeply we look into it, the more surprising it becomes. I think the first thing we have to realize is that the doctor is not really interested in persuading us to do anything. At the very best and most optimistic view the doctor wants to simply make us well and happy. If that is achieved the job is done. We go to see the doctor because we don't feel well and happy and the doctor may make us well and happy, so we go in the hope that this will be achieved. Therefore there is a common goal at the outset. Perhaps, before we try any persuasion, we should consider the common goal we can achieve with our subject. If it is clear that they will leave the transaction better off than they went into it, a lot of the tension is removed.

There is a lot of froth and bubble about giving the customer what they want and satisfying needs, but there is a good chance our subject has no idea what they want or need. They may know that they don't feel well or happy, or they may think that they know what will make them feel well and happy, but they are often wrong and it is our understanding and interpretation that gives us the power to persuade. Yes, in every situation! If Mr Perkins, buyer for Bogitts Homes, thinks he needs a sharper price on facing bricks, what he really wants is approval, recognition, and acknowledgement from his bosses. If you can get him that, he won't care much what he pays for the bricks.

Does That Hurt?

We fall over one day and realize we have broken our arm. We are certain this is the case because of the pain, our friends' view of the situation and the fact that we shouldn't have two elbows on the same arm. This prompts us to see the doctor.

"Good morning, what seems to be the trouble," she says (a nice opening open-investigating question).

"I think I have broken my arm."

Now imagine the doctor had been reading sales training books – clearly there is an opportunity for a deal. A problem has been suggested and can soon be turned into a decision by strong benefit statements.

"Oh boy, do I have an opportunity for you! What we intend to do is to amputate your left leg and the exciting thing is that I can guarantee a 50% drop in sock washing costs!"

There are a couple of sinister flies paddling about in this particular ointment. Firstly the customer was interested in their arm. If all we do is legs, we are a bit stuffed despite our verbal dexterity. Secondly, while the benefit or even incentive may be a fifty percent reduction in a certain cost, it cannot compensate for the pain and loss of the offered solution. Let's get back to the real doctor.

"I think I've broken my arm."

This statement must suggest a need – well surely the need must be treatment for the broken arm – but not so fast. As we have already seen it is never a good idea to offer your solution too fast.

"You think you've broken it? How did this happen?"

"I fell over the cat."

"Really? Pets can cause so much trouble, can't they. When did this happen?"

"About three days ago."

"And when did it go this colour?"

"Almost straight away."

"Did that hurt?"

"Yaroo!"

"Hmm, I think you're right, you may have broken your arm, but just to be sure I am sending you to the hospital for an X-ray. When I get the results back, we will decide on the best treatment."

What you have here is that, even when the customer thinks they have identified the problem and the solution they believe they want and need, the skilled practitioner continues with their investigation until the absolutely correct diagnosis and solution are found.

Try to think as a doctor would when you meet these subjects. Have no preconceived ideas of what solutions, products, or services you wish to offer, and don't be misled by what they initially state that they think they want or need. Patiently take notes and check back on possible grey areas by asking questions. Apart from anything else, it will make you appear important and professional which goes a long way towards persuasion before you even start persuading – if you know what I mean.

POINTS TO PONDER ON CHAPTER 12

1. Understand how valuable it is to put on a show.

2. Just because you are good at something doesn't mean you are guaranteed to succeed. If you can't build the surrounding experience around your skill or product, you could still fail.

3. If the customer sees too big a problem, no amount of benefits will ever outweigh it.

4. Sometimes you will need to make the problem bigger before the subject can appreciate the value of the solution.

5. Don't be afraid to be nice.

6. Don't always accept the subject's diagnosis of their own problem.

7. To get to know your subject well enough to put on a good show, questioning skills become even more important.

PART THREE

ARE WE THERE YET?

CHAPTER 13: RESISTANCE IS FUTILE
In which we discover how to tell if someone is interested even when they say they are not – and how we overcome all resistance

CHAPTER 14: THE PRESSURE GAME
In which we examine persuasion techniques that may be described as high pressure, but then don't we need a little pressure to succeed?

CHAPTER 15: BIG DECISIONS
In which we discover whether our subject is being persuaded to make a major or minor decision

CHAPTER 16: MEASURING SUCCESS
In which we discover how, in a small decision, a simple 'yes' is all we need for success, but in more complicated decisions it is very hard to know exactly where we are

CHAPTER 17: IT'S A REAL BARGAIN
In which we discover the to and fro, the cut and thrust, and the pure fun that is bargaining

CHAPTER 18: EVERYTHING'S NEGOTIABLE
In which we learn that there is much more to negotiation than simple bargaining

CHAPTER 19: PERSUASIVE MARKETING
In which we find the subjects for our persuasive talents and build their expectations

CHAPTER 13

RESISTANCE IS FUTILE

In which we discover how to tell if someone is interested even when they say they're not – and how we overcome all resistance

The old timers can help us to spot those drool moments. They developed a nose for what they called 'buying signals'. The theory is that as the 'prospect' becomes more convinced in their head, they start to exhibit outward, recognizable signs that they are ready to buy. This old and neglected art is actually quite useful because these signals can be slight and subtle, and can sometimes be downright contradictory. On an obvious level they can start to ask more detailed questions about the minutiae or the care or maintenance of your offer. "A pet polar bear, eh? What exactly do they eat?"

Always remember that it is a good idea to be suspicious of people who appear to like what you are saying. When you view something you have no intention of buying it is so easy just to say, "How lovely. I like the ornate handles. I've got a bit more shopping to do so we may pop back later on." And then we, like idiots, write "Very interested" in our report, but of course the reverse is nearly always true. If someone says something tough or discouraging about our offer they may be genuinely 'very interested' or they may really hate us and want us to go away. This is where the thick skin is required.

Come with Me to The Kasbah

Look for a moment at the psychology involved if you go into a Middle Eastern souk market. You are on holiday there, you have read the guide book on how to bargain and you want one of those tasseled hats that will make you look like a prat. You have probably asked your fellow tourists and at your hotel for a guide to the best shop and likely prices. You casually pick up said pratty hat and toss it nonchalantly about in your hands with a carefully applied look of boredom and as the stallholder approaches you put it down and pick up a wooden snake.

"Good morning, please come into my shop and drink tea with me."

No, it's a trap!

"No thank you, I've got to get on," you say, nonchalantly replacing the snake and walking away. Then with a beautiful piece of thespian choreography you happen to remember a butterfly of a last thought. "Oh yes, by the way, how much are the Fezzes?"

"Come, come, come in! These are the finest in the whole city, but I will fix you the best price."

"I haven't got the time now; I just want a guide price."

He produces a calculator (they always produce a calculator), "Come, come and sit down. I will produce a special low price for you."

Actually a terrific sale is happening here and you are now the helpless fly tangled beyond escape, but let's just imagine our market trader boobs a little bit (they never do, actually...) and gives you a price. "They are 200 shekels."

"Poo. Ridiculous. I will give you ten!"

"Ten, sir! I will be ruined at ten. That's a mere fraction of what I pay..."

And so it goes on, but look around – every other idiot is wearing a stupid tasseled hat. That is what the tourists buy and the stallholder has been making a good living from them for fifty years. What he sees is a perfect exhibition of what, in his line of work, are classic buying signals. In other words, after a bit of time experience will tell you that, despite outward appearance, certain signs and activity give the game away when people are really interested.

Look for The Clues

In our life back home, when our subject becomes tricky, disparages our offer, or makes outrageous demands, this can actually be a deal breaker because we fail to recognize the buying signal when it actually bites us in the bottom. When you go to view that new television which the advertisement in the Press had led you to believe you could buy for £400, the salesperson wows you with high definition, black-to-black contrast, and high-speed motion. "How much?" you enquire, feeling in your pocket for the credit cards. "This one is on offer at £3800." Of course a lot of people will rush about screaming, but lots more nod sagely and pretend that although this offers exceptional value they need to just do a little more research before making a decision and then creep away.

It is a shame that we don't do enough work to reveal our subject's true thoughts and feelings, but the buying signals should give us some clues. The classics are, if we are asked very specific questions about price, delivery, guarantee, or product care, we can get a few 'what if' questions such as, "What if we wanted to change it?", "What if it broke down?", then we could get 'how to use it' questions. Couples will start to confer with each other, even nodding, smiling, and possibly saying, "We'll take it!" (It's rarely that easy.)

If Only

I will now reveal a power word. Its real territory is in negotiating, but it also has quite a bit of clout in the sale. That word is 'IF' and when combined with 'THEN' its effects are atomic. It's like going bear hunting and arriving at a dark cave mouth. You could rush from the sunlight into the blackness with a stick shouting, "Come on bear, if you think you're hard enough", a course of action that I would deem foolhardy and potentially fatal in a kind of angry bear-gory sort of way. Personally, I would advocate standing well back and throwing in small rocks from a safe distance. 'If' and 'Then' are just such little rocks that we can toss into the subject's cave without danger of a terminal outcome. The old pro's called them 'trial closes' but they do all sorts of good things for the persuasion process.

"Can this be delivered by next Tuesday?"

A simple request and may be a buying signal. A mere mortal may be tempted to say, "Yep!" That is a wasted opportunity. Just watch the steely-eyed old professional.

"Tuesday. If I can get it delivered by Tuesday then could you proceed with the order today?"

This does so many good things I hardly know where to start. First, using 'If' makes an offer that can be withdrawn without killing the deal. What 'If' does is put a condition into place.

"I see the price on the windscreen. Can I have a discount?"

"If we arranged a discount, then would you be in a position to purchase this car today?"

"Not today, I have to sell my old car."

"Then sit down and we will discuss what can be done."

The discount is off the table with no offence. The customer could honestly not fulfill the conditions. We tend to blunder about offering concessions without conditions.

"What's the maximum discount?"

"10%."

"Can you deliver Tuesday?"

"Yep."

"Is there interest free credit?"

"Yep."

"Is there three year's free servicing?"

"Yep."

"OK. I think that's all the information I need. I will get back to you."

And what's really annoying is that if after months they do finally decide to buy, they will expect all those concessions to still be on the table. So always always try and answer a request for a concession with a condition expressed by 'If' and 'Then'.

"Is there three year's free servicing?"

"If you choose a car today from our current stock, then I believe that offer is still available. Are you ready to order today?"

The next thing it does in the rock-in-the-bear-cave thing is that it can flush out the subject's true intentions without causing too much upset.

"If we offered as much as 10% discount, then could you proceed today?"

"Well I need authority from my boss."

Yes, disappointing, but a lot more useful than "very interested".

It is also an offer we can withdraw.

"If you want it by Tuesday, then I will need cash upfront."

"No, I don't think we can do that, we will need to use credit."

"Then it will probably have to be Wednesday or Thursday."

It also gets commitment from the subject.

"If we can organize interest-free credit, then could you give me an order?"

"Yes, I think so."

"Ok, let's get some coffee while we organize the paperwork."

The danger of it not being a condition can be illustrated with a cheery exercise. During a quiet relaxed moment with a group of work colleagues, say, "Brian, give me your watch" and then remain completely silent with no explanation.

When they hand it over (even after some protest or request for reasons which you ignore), which they usually do, just put it in your pocket and carry on with your life. A free watch! People have a weird habit of responding to requests that are made confidently with no conditions.

A Condition of Purchase

In the early days, this persuasion thing was seen as a bit of a pressure business. The proponents developed the senses and attitude of predatory hunters, therefore it stood to reason that when the prey was cornered you could expect a bit of a fight. You poke said angry bear with the pointy stick of trial closes and it will respond with the slashing claws of objection!

Their theory (not mine) was quite simply this. You ask someone to buy something. They say no – why have they said no, because they have some objection to saying yes. If that is, "I don't need one", "I don't want one", "Why on earth would I want one of these", you probably cocked up the A.I.D.A. big time. You have their attention, they are interested, and you have kindled the fires of desire. Then the objection will be, "I can't afford it", "I need to think about it", "How much!", "I don't like that colour". Clearly, if the objection is preventing them from buying, the simple expedient of removing or dealing with that objection will result, or so the theory goes, in an inevitable sale. There is one let-out and that is a condition which clearly prevents a sale.

"So when would you like to take the new mountain bike?"

"I haven't got any legs!"

"When would you envisage investing in expansion?"

"This company is bankrupt – I'm the liquidator."

But you won't get off that easy. If you had qualified the prospect you wouldn't have got this far before finding a condition this late on in the process.

Objection, Your Honour

The salespeople had a golf bag full of objection techniques but which, on the whole, are so slick it makes me uneasy. However, here are a few for now and we can discuss our nerves later.

Setting the objection aside has a number of good effects. "I think this is going to cost too much!"

"Listen I so want you to enjoy wearing this crown that price is not going to be an issue. Let's just forget the money for a moment and talk about why you would enjoy being King."

Or, more blatantly and simply, "Forget the price for a moment. Is this exactly the one you wanted?"

"Let's talk about the money later. I think you will be pleasantly surprised. Anyway I won't let you lose this opportunity over a daft thing like money."

Let's move into the psychology of the subject for a moment. If it was you and you were clinging to the last straw thought of, "Oh no, if I don't stop this here, I'm going to buy something in haste…", before you are lost, you would chuck out an ill-thought-out, "Can't afford it." By setting that aside we can find out if there is a deep objection or doubt. It may be time to return to a bit more desire-building. Often in these cases, when the juices are made to flow vigorously enough, the original objection is forgotten.

Also remember that we are working a fairly strict system here, one that, by setting aside an objection that we are not ready for, puts our subject back on our map.

Work with Me Here

Next we can agree with our subject's objection but with a bit of subtle rewording. The key here is, whatever you do don't disagree. The customer is always right even when they are wrong.

"Heavens, that's expensive."

"I agree. It would be a major investment."

Here it comes… "But I'm sure you would agree that it is important for a person of your status to possess items that reflect your elevated position".

If the subject is driven by bigoted prejudice: "All sales-people are liars."

"You are right to be suspicious. I wouldn't imagine that you have achieved your current position without being careful and that is precisely why my employers offer a unique, no quibble, guarantee."

Get in First

If you know there is something about your offer that the customer may object to and it worries you, don't try and hide it but get your retaliation in first. "I bet when you look at this you will be asking how we can build it at the price. By investing in modern production and by not fitting unwanted extras, we can offer exceptional value for money." (We don't say cheap, they may think it but we don't say it.)

It's not a bad idea to test the objection validity that can lead to surprisingly useful answers.

What Do You Mean, Too Expensive?

"No, that's far too expensive."

"I'm sorry but how do you mean too expensive?"

You could get:

"Compared to the shop next door."

"If we match their price, will you then wish to go ahead?"

Or:

"It's good value but I don't have the money."

"If we can show you how you can afford it, then can we go ahead?

Or:

"I just said that to get you off my back."

"I'm so sorry; I clearly failed to explain myself properly."

Or;

"All that money for a wheel."

"No! You get the whole car!"

You will notice that every time an objection is investigated, a little commitment question is shoved in there. This can be used at any point in the sales process. For instance the subject asks a question like, "Have you got a red one?"

If you have got a red one, don't say "Yep", ask, "A red one, is that important to you? Or, "Did you particularly want a red one?" If they say, "yes", you reply, "That'll be thirty quid, please. Would you like it wrapped?"

They Know It is Dangerous

If you sell products that are outrageously expensive, big, or dangerous, you know it, the subject knows it, so (and this is a dodgy concept) you can ignore the objection.

"How much are your snow tigers?"

"A million quid."

"Crumbs, that's a lot."

You give a knowing smile, "Big, isn't it."

A vestige of a nod, "It bit me!"

"They do that!"

These are not objections. They are observations If your subject is buying something outrageous from you they will like to say so. "This car I'm buying off you cost more than my first home."

You are a fellow conspirator not an opponent. But now things start to get really tough, "I want to think it over."

"Of course you do, I would want to think over such a big decision. However, when people say that they want to think things over, there is clearly something that they are not sure about. That is entirely my fault. What is it about my offer that I failed to explain? What are you not sure about?"

"Well, I don't think it would fit up my stairs."

"OK, I can understand that. If I could demonstrate that it will fit up your stairs, can you OK the agreement today?"

The Words That We Choose

Notice that re-wording again. The salespeople of yore discovered political correctness about a hundred years before the chattering classes did. You can change words that, on the face of it, don't change the meaning but change the emotional impact. I'm not a disruptive influence, I'm an agent for change! She's not a tart, she operates with negotiable hospitality. Don't sign a contract, OK an agreement. We don't buy – we own and use. It isn't smelly, it's pre-scented. It's not expensive, it's premium quality. It is not a cost, it is an investment. Spinning before the word was even thought of!

POINTS TO PONDER ON CHAPTER 13

1. When they say "no" they may mean "maybe". Watch any market trader.

2. Customers can afford to be nice when they are really going to walk away without buying.

3. Don't be afraid of objections, deal with them.

4. Don't make concessions without conditions.

5. Choose your words carefully.

CHAPTER 14

THE PRESSURE GAME

In which we examine persuasion techniques that may be described as high pressure, but then don't we need a little pressure to succeed?

Some persuasion techniques could be seen as representing pressure – the prospect is not going to get away easily. No one in today's world would buy a book called *The High Pressure Salespersons' Handbook* but can I play devil's advocate for a moment. Why wouldn't they? Tell me exactly what is wrong with a bit of pressure? Who are you and why are you reading this book?

Maybe you are reading this book to just be a more persuasive person. If that is the case you will notice that these simple formulas give a structure and intent. Most people do not conduct intentional conversations that are planned to achieve a defined outcome – cold, calculating, maybe, but that's what is needed to stay in control. I think that I'm quite a reasonable chess player but my son bought me a fiendish pocket chess computer. When the game starts, if you really concentrate, you can get this thing on the run but as you tire and think of other things, this beastly thing starts to get up to stuff. It has its plan and it relentlessly works it. I get whupped nearly every time and only by uninterrupted concentration and attention can I beat it. It's not clever, it's persistent and single minded – try a bit of that and transform your life.

Maybe you're a super salesperson who negotiates mega deals on a global basis. Examine your last half dozen commercial conversations – did you have a clear destination in mind, did you know where your subject was as regards to being persuaded, and did you come away with clear and measurable progress towards what you wanted (*not* V. Interested). How was your PowerPoint show – did it work A.I.D.A.? I bet it didn't.

Or perhaps you are reading this book because you have a small business, or things that you need more yes's to in order to make a decent living. Well, forget all the moral judgments and intellectual arguments and take these little statements from the past on board: **'PRODUCTION MINUS SALES EQUALS SCRAP'**; or, **'NOTHING HAPPENS UNTIL SOMEONE SELLS SOMETHING'**. If nothing else, take the section on A.I.D.A. at face value and work it as it is, as a script, and just like the crude old salespeople of old, your sales will increase beyond your wildest dreams. Once you are rich and happy you can do 'subtle'. Just for starters, go out and ask people to buy things – and that takes us nicely to closing techniques.

Check Before Closing

The whole point of the exercise, in truth this book itself, is to get a positive and anticipated outcome from interaction with another person. We have detected some buying signals and we have dealt with the objections. Just before we actually get the decision that we want, we must clear the decks of our debris or wreckage from the preliminary skirmishes. So a quick check through moves us forward nicely to our goal. A mental checklist will make sure things are ready to close.

 ⌐ Did I hear and completely understand the obstacles that are in the other person's mind?

⌡ Did I put it back into the subject's court so they understand that we understand?

⌡ Has the obstacle been removed?

⌡ Does the subject agree that the obstacle has been removed?

If you have done that, don't hang about as it's time to ask for a decision.

Silence is Golden

A tool to use to increase pressure is silence. On the closer's tool bag is engraved the legendary "The first one to speak loses!" Try it, you will sweat with anxiety but grit your teeth and with the result put the closing question and shut up.

Choices, Choices

A good basic close is the 'Alternative'. Put quite simply, if people are given two choices they will most likely take one of the ones you offer rather than going to the trouble of making up a third one of their own. The problem is that most of us give people the choice of 'yes' or 'no'.

"Do you need any help?", "Are you ready to order?", "Do you want one of these?"

We have to offer the choice, "Do you want to do business with me? Or would you like to do business with...me?"

For instance, "Did you want the red...or the blue?", "Can you manage that for now... or would you like it delivered?"

If you run a café or restaurant you can pay for your luxury holiday simply by getting your waiting staff to stop saying, "Will there be anything else?" and start saying, "Would you like sweet or coffee?"

A Prickly Customer

The Hedgehog or Boomerang close is a classic persuasion technique – you throw questions back as if they were prickly hedgehogs which you return quickly as soon as you catch them!

"Do these come in size six?"

"Do you particularly want one in a six? Take a seat and I will see if I can find you one." (Only do this if you do actually have a size six!)

The Exaggeration close:

"OK, shall I put you down for 400 cases?"

"400! Are you mad – we would be lucky to use 10."

"Okey dokey, ten it is. Could you just OK the agreement?"

The Assumption close:

"OK, I think that's everything. We'll get it delivered for you next week."

How Much is That Doggy in The window

The Puppy Dog close is an oldie but a goodie. Imagine that I walk up to you and ask you to buy a puppy – that is probably the last thing on this earth that you currently want. But imagine one morning that you open your front door and there is a box and when you open it a little doe-eyed pup washes your face with doggy kisses. Obviously it belongs to somebody and you make an effort to find the owner, but in the meantime you have given this little chap a name, "Bonzo", and after six months you have got kind of attached to each other. Then the phone call comes. "Hey, you didn't find a dog, did you?" "Yes I did, we've called him Bonzo." "Oh, that's fantastic. Could you return him to me." "But we love him." You would pay anything to keep him – the sale has been made. Legend has it that in the early days of colour TV in the USA, the price was so prohibitive and the technology so poorly understood that the sets were almost impossible to sell. A shrewd operator started giving them away in the interests of "research". So a free TV, no strings attached, you just send it back after three months. Of course ninety percent of people ended up buying the TV. That is the Puppy Dog close.

There is one close that, in my researches into the dusty old sales books, inevitably mentions a wise old man and is variously called the 'Benjamin Franklin', the 'Churchill', the 'Cromwell' or the 'Archimedes', but the theme is the same. You say to the subject, "I can clearly see that you are torn by this decision so let's see how wise old Rasputin (or whoever) would do it. We make two lists – one positive and one negative; clearly if the positives outweigh the negatives than you would be right to go ahead. Don't you agree?" Long, long silence. "I suppose so."

"Great! Let's look at our decision – to drink a whole bottle of whisky."

✓ **Positives** – Happiness, forget troubles, feel more confident, partner more attractive, and tell boss where to get off, feel invincible.

✓ **Negatives** – Arrested, disgraced, alcohol poisoning.

"Clearly the positives outweigh the negatives so let's get drinking!"

I am being a bighead here, because as I check these closing techniques I start to think they are cheesy and nasty so I don't take them entirely seriously, but for years they worked. I see the Ben Franklin and think, "No one would fall for that", but they did and they still do. It is like the Gordian knot that challenged the greatest minds until Alexander just slashed through it with a sword. Crude, but effective.

These old salespeople also had some brass nerve and sometimes I avoid their techniques simply because I lack their courage. For instance, I dare you to try this: "I think we need to examine our budget before we proceed."

"I can appreciate that, but are you just saying that because you want to get rid of me?" Then silence... Phew, a bit strong even for me.

If you are worried about this pressure thing, there is a test you can apply. It will on the one hand settle your discomfort about the pressure and on the other hand will challenge you to be a bit more deliberate with your life.

Bringing Home The Bacon

But first a story. I spend a huge percentage of my time getting companies to focus on their customers, customer care, customer satisfaction, but where does that make money? I was walking along a country lane when I met a farmer I knew leaning on a gate.

"'ello, Geoff," he calls.

"Hello, Farmer Giles," I called back. I noticed that this farmer was accompanied by a huge pig. The farmer lovingly scratched the pig's head, "'ello, Rosie, old girl!" The pig, grunting contentedly, started to vigorously nuzzle the farmer's pocket. "What are you up to, old girl? You knows I got an apple in there, don't you?" whereupon he produced a large red apple which he gave to the pig who consumed it with juicy enthusiasm. "You loves your apple, don't you old girl," he said, kissing the pig on the head. Then turning to me, he said, "She's a lovely pig, Rosie is, she's going off to be bacon next week aren't you girl?"

I was stunned. "You mean you are going to kill her?"

"Well of course. I'm a pig farmer. I don't keep pet pigs!"

"So why are you nice to it?"

"I love my pigs. The people up the road battery breed their pigs in crowded dark sheds. The animals are so stressed that they bite off their own tails. You get awful meat from them."

I suppose it is the same with us – customer care is vital. See what happens to companies who treat customers badly, but on the other hand we don't want pet customers, we have to make our bacon.

A Loving Relationship

Stripping this down to its basic components we have two elements that are vital.

- ↵ **The relationship**. Whoever we are trying to persuade, it is necessary to have a good relationship with them. Being nice, making concessions, giving gifts, treating them well, making them feel rewarded and appreciated, all build a relationship.

J **Our interests**. You read this book, you work, you own a business, and you make profits to take care of your interests. We would like to learn to persuade in order to take care of our interests.

To have a rich, prosperous, happy life that is supported by your ability to persuade, one cannot conflict with the other. If your relationship-building damages your interests, that is plain stupid.

"Take my advice – don't pay the extra for my product. My competitor is not only cheaper, they are better."

Conversely, "I know it doesn't work and the product is poor, but I've got your money so ha-ha, you get stuffed!"

Therefore if I recommended applying electric shocks to the subject until they agree, it would be legitimate as long as they left saying, "What a brilliant experience. I am more than happy to repeat it."

The conclusion must be that high pressure which damages future transactions is not worthwhile. As potential targets, be warned that timeshare sales, cannibals, vampires, and double glazing salespeople have no intention of ever seeing you again – especially if they see you first.

I Rest My Case, M'lud

That kind of wraps it up for dear old A.I.D.A., but before we move on to higher and more subtle territory, consider how the A.I.D.A. structure can be applied.

I used to criticize A.I.D.A. because it was a bit of a blunt instrument; I felt that a fine scalpel of targeted persuasion would be better than A.I.D.A.'s sledgehammer. The danger, I always felt, was that without detailed knowledge of the subject you could be way wide of the mark. What I neglected to realize was that my day job, which entails talking convincingly to audiences of hundreds and even thousands, gave me no opportunity for such precise targeting.

The persuasion of crowds or groups responds very well to this simple structure.

The Barrister's final address:

"Ladies and Gentlemen of the Jury, do you have children? (Attention)

How would you feel if this monster did this to one of your children? (Interest)

Would you not want to see justice done? (Desire)

Therefore I will ask you to go away now and find this person guilty as charged." (Action)

Next time you hear a speech or a presentation, whisper under your breath, "So what" and "What's in it for me" and in future correct your own presentation accordingly.

POINTS TO PONDER ON CHAPTER 14

1. Before moving into the closing stages, make sure there are absolutely no misunderstandings on either side by checking before closing.

2. When you ask for the decision, remember the enormous power of silence.

3. If you give the person a choice, make sure all the choices are positive for you.

4. Do good things to build the relationship but remember you are doing that to take care of your interests.

5. Make sure there is no conflict between building the relationship and taking care of your interests.

6. If you benefit from the outcome of your persuasion, make sure you understand what is in it for the other party.

CHAPTER **15**

BIG DECISIONS

In which we discover whether our subject
is being persuaded to make a major or
minor decision

I suppose you could call the more elementary persuasion techniques 'Pounce and Sign' and they work extremely well if the decision is not a major one nor has the threat of serious consequences. However, we can come up against real resistance when the decision is a huge one. It's not about whether the other party likes or even dislikes us, it is when they can see that their decisions could have life-changing ramifications. If we are going to use our map analogy here, our subjects are a very long way from the destination that we have got planned for them, but I believe that anyone can be persuaded to do anything. After all, the only thing that is preventing them is the processes that are going on in their head.

If you watch the current batch of superstar illusionists they seem to be able to alter the audience's entire perception of the world. The difference is that after they've convinced us that we have lost the use of our legs, or they can talk to the dead or read our minds, they give a little chuckle and put the world back to rights. We, on the other hand, are looking for permanent changes, changes that we have to bear responsibility for, so before we turn up the gas too much we have to consider the consequences. Should this person have married you? Should this company change their supplier of fifty years and put their faith in you? Can you really look after this person's life savings?

When I was a lot younger my persuasion skills were raw but natural. I persuaded as a sort of reflex to any challenge or situation, and as a result I got myself and everyone around me into very regrettable scrapes. First step, then, is to ask yourself, "Do I really want this and can I manage the responsibility and consequences?"

I Know Where I am Going

That being dealt with, let's go for it! Seeing the overview of the whole journey is the first key step.

- ⋃ Who are you going to persuade?
- ⋃ What is it you are going to persuade them to do?
- ⋃ Where exactly are they now?
- ⋃ Where exactly do you want them to be?
- ⋃ What obstacles stand between these two clearly defined positions?

If you are in a business, choose someone out of your head who you would dearly like to do business with. OK, you've chosen Mr Perkins of Perkins International Transport. That is a very ambitious choice: Perkins would be bigger than any other client you have ever had, you have dealt with Mr Perkins before and he hates you, he is quite happy with his current supplier, and you are going to struggle on price. Grim as this sounds, it is actually worse than this because in the real world you don't even know all the facts stated – but now we do know them, and if that is the complete list, once these obstacles have been removed Perkins is ours. This in commercial circles is known as 'Targeted Selling'. If handled correctly, the outcome should be inevitable even if the process takes years.

Major or Minor?

I think here it would be useful to understand where a major decision differs from a minor one. Once we understand that, we should be able to travel vigorously in both directions. Understanding the major decisions should give us mastery of the technique needed to drive them to your advantage but once the checks have been applied, we should also realize that everything else is a minor decision – and we could have much happier and more prosperous lives if we simply ask for more of them. "Can I please read your newspaper?", "Do you want that piano in your garden?", "Fancy an early night?", "Stuff work, shall we go to the cinema?", "May I have a little more please?", "Could you let me have the money now?" The only technique being used here is just a bit of child-like confidence. The major decisions can be recognized by the following:

- ✓ The decision may take some considerable time, sometimes even years. If it is big enough, don't give up. I had one client who refused to even see me for six years so I started sending him anniversary cards and a bottle of champagne. I wrote on the card, "Congratulations! You have resisted me for another year!" Risky, but what the heck – I got that deal and it was very worth the wait.

- ✓ It is unlikely that an immediate purchase will be made. Here we have a dilemma. As previously stated, if we let the subject be "Very interested" and "Think it over" all is lost, but we can hardly expect a multi-million pound deal signed during a preliminary 5-minute visit. The answer is for you to stay in control of the process – which leads us neatly to the next point.

- ✓ This suggests that more than one meeting will be required. We need to set out to control the time and place of these meetings.

- ✓ Often more than one person is involved in the decision. The sinister thing for us is that we don't always know that, and we should do our utmost to find out who they are and if possible address them in person.

ↄ The subject will be cautious because a mistake would have major repercussions. The truth is that the current situation is our biggest competitor even if doing nothing could result in dreadful consequences for their organization.

No Decision, No Blame

A dear American friend told me this very challenging story. When he was young, he was a fiery ambitious person who had founded an insurance company in his early twenties. He had driven it on in the way only the energy of youth could, to the point that it became a thorn in the side of a huge insurance corporation. Their solution was to buy him out for millions and give him a minor seat on the board. I think they hoped he would take his winnings and go surfing all day but no, he wanted to be involved. So they kept finding projects to get rid of him and one was this: on their books they had an agricultural insurance company which didn't fit with their motor, life, and home business.

"Go and sell it," they told my chum.

"For how much?"

"You will be doing well if you get 20 million."

He went off to the centre of the USA where agriculture is a big deal and found a buyer. The battle was long and hard but he squeezed this buyer until at last they offered 25 million. He rushed to the phone full of excitement to ring his home office.

"Guess what I've got an offer of 25 million."

"Well, if they will offer that it must be worth more to them. Tell them we don't move for less than thirty."

When he went back to the buyer with that, they basically threw him out along with the deal. So the agriculture insurance company was kept on the books until over the years it managed to lose over a hundred million and was wound up with the loss of many jobs So whose fault was that? Well guess what? It was nobody's If you spoke to the board they would say, "Ah yes, the old agricultural business – victim of changing times, very sad, tried to find a buyer years back but no one would pay the price. Some young gun wasted a lot of time on that one."

See? No one is to blame! If they had accepted the offer someone would have had to make a decision. What if the company had made millions in other hands – who would be blamed? The person who made the decision? No decision, no blame – however horrible the consequences. Have a look at politicians, relations, and bureaucrats – does it frustrate you when they don't even seem to see common sense. Well now you know why.

Exposed

In my own experience, when I was young, naïve, and over enthusiastic (none of which I am now), I was representing a technical product which I knew was brilliant. I had targeted a client who had great need for our product and was paying too much for something inferior. In the bag, then, you would think, but I was totally stone-walled by the buyer. I found the reason was simple; the current supplier was blatantly bribing the buyer and had been for years. I told my boss who flew into a rage and stormed off to see their CEO to expose the nasty plot. The buyer disappeared and I sailed in to see the new, hopefully honest, buyer. I was met by the CEO himself who, looking most downcast, told me that he had been shocked by the revelation but his current supplier who he had used for years had explained that it was all down to the wicked machinations of the buyer, so he was, after chastening them for their foolishness, going to stick by them... "But we've got a better product than the people who have, in effect, been stealing from you for years!"

"That is as maybe, but better the devil you know, and anyway I don't appreciate people who tell tales out of school. Good day to you!"

We never did business with them ever, but a few years later they went bust (he he).

Lessons learnt. Firstly, don't ever be the bearer of bad news; we have to learn very subtle ways of letting people discover truths for themselves. Secondly, people would rather stay in a bad place than suffer the pain and risk of change.

All Change

The essence of this entire book is about getting people to change. From no to yes, from I hate you to I love you, from I don't want it to I do want it. We are setting out to persuade them to change their mind. Of course the bigger the decision, the more work will have to be done to achieve that change. One of the biggest obstacles, as you can now see, is the subject's current position, however perilous.

When I speak to my audiences, one of my party tricks is to challenge them to change. I tell them that they fear change and that they could not change a tiny aspect of their life. Then comes the challenge (try it for yourself), from this day forward, sit in a different chair to watch TV. I bet you have given a little chuckle at that but I also bet that you won't do it!

Someone said that real change is not possible until the pain of not changing outweighs the pain of changing. You would soon move if I set fire to your chair.

Therefore we have to increase the peril and dissatisfaction without obviously being the one who did it. What larks we'll have!

Dissatisfaction Guaranteed

What is it that we want the subject to be dissatisfied with, feel threatened by or in peril from? It is where they currently are now, their position, or situation. On our map of persuasion stick a pin right now where our subject really is in relation to where we would like them to be. You don't know?

Well one of the key jobs will be to find out. A phase of thorough investigation before all else.

There is a danger here, that whilst it is important that we find out as much as possible about our subject, their current position and our opportunities to create dissatisfaction with it, they may not enjoy this process of intimate examination. So we must do this in a subtle and gentle way – a cheery chat that you will both enjoy. The only difference is that while you both chuckle away at the fripperies and fluttering butterflies of social interaction your razor honed mind is collecting information.

Here is a tip. I have a mind like a sieve – razor sharp or not, a goldfish could wipe the floor with me on fact retention, so I take notes. You would think it would wind the other person up and I suppose it would if you are a klutz but if you can write things down with a chuckle because you want to preserve their pearls of wisdom for posterity and because you are taking them seriously, it actually helps.

"Yes, yes, you are so right. Let me just make a note of that."

The old timers used to start an interview by getting out an order form and using the replies to fill in the details. When complete, a simple "I think that's everything. If you could just put your monika 'ere, I'll be on me way!" (I know, I break out in a sweat at the thought of it too, but it worked for those of the thicker hide…)

Living in The Past

A slightly more gentle form of interrogation is to invite the subject to talk about the past. For some reason people are much more comfortable about the past than they are about the future. Questions about the future can seem intrusive. Of course it's the future and their activities in it that we are interested in but a gentle transition from past to future can be achieved and loads of yummy facts come out.

"Where did you go for your holiday last year?"

"Majorca."

"Did you enjoy it?" (A closed question, I know, but a vital one. This is a fork in our road.)

"No."

To which we ask, "Oh I'm sorry to hear that. What actually was the problem?"

Or,

"Yes it was great!"

"Oh brilliant. What was it that was so nice", and so on – you get the idea, but where it leads to is, "So is that the kind of holiday you want this year?"

Guess what you are selling…

Down to Brass Tacks

Now we know where they buy from, their status, the other people involved, the current process and Uncle Tom Cobley – all we need to start persuading.

I have a dilemma here because very powerful commercial persuasion programmes are based on a model that I am not entirely content about. I can see the logic, and this system works for me time and time again. I will reveal its skills and powers in a moment, but first my concerns. The idea is that every purchase or decision is made to solve a problem. By identifying the problem a solution can be sold to solve the problem. Some bright spark came up with the concept of 'Solution Selling' which the marketing people loved to death, so everything now has to be something or other solution. It's not Fred's Removals, it's Frederick's Logistic Solutions; not plumbers, it's Aquifer Transferable Solutions; every lorry you see has 'solutions' written on it somewhere.

Someone slightly more savvy realized that simply finding a problem and then eagerly offering to solve it didn't always result in the enthusiastic snatching of the arm that was expected. I also believe that you can persuade people to do huge and dramatic things when they have absolutely no problem at all, but for now it's problem time.

The Problems are Growing

We know exactly where the other person is and their position on our map. We must invite them on their journey with us and our products. Apparently an understanding of a customer is not just about finding out their current position but is about understanding the problems they will encounter moving forward – and then to offer solutions to these problems with our product or service. The classic old sales description of this process is called 'identifying the customer's needs'. The bluebottle in this ointment is that the subject rarely has a clear idea of what they need.

On a very simple but useful level, a very basic bit of verbal dexterity can be quite profitable If you offer car repairs, a potential customer may say, "I have to go everywhere by bus since the engine fell out of my car and I can't afford to fix it."

You may say, "We can fix it cheap!"

That may elicit a "So what", or a "Yes but", because the customer didn't say they had a problem or need, or a problem that could be converted into a need. You see we have to conduct some simple alchemy here turning the base metal of general whinging into the gold of a solid need. Try this, it's easy.

"So what are you saying? Is it that you need your car fixing at an affordable price?" You have turned a suggested need into a real need.

Try this as an exercise. Every whinge you hear, try Geoff's patented 'Whingomatic' converter and try and turn the moan into needs.

"Cor, my piles are giving me gip!"

"Would you like a treatment that could give you some relief?"

"My boss is a pain in the neck."

"Are you looking for someone who could silence him permanently?"

Note: they are always questions and they convert statements of a situation into statements of a need.

It's Never as Easy as It Seems

You may well have brilliant products that are well priced and you just know that if your subject bought them their problems would instantly be solved – and they would be happy forever. So tell me this, why are any of your competitors still in business? Oh, I know, you are working to complete capacity and they are taking up the slack? No? Is it because you know in reality what you offer is a bit inferior (because if it is get that fixed now, 'persuasion' won't save you). It's not that? Then it is because your prospects don't have the correct perception of the value of your offering. The bane of my life is the keen 'teccy' because they think solely in gee whizz solutions. Their conversations are filled with a puppy-like eagerness which actually scares the prospect.

"Can it do calculations?"

"Easy peasy. They all do that!"

"We have a big payroll each week."

"No probs, it can do payroll standing on its head!"

"We employ 500 people all with different hours and wage rates."

"That wouldn't bother it; it could calculate the wages for everyone on the planet. A laptop could do that!"

So why isn't the sales model a problem expressed and a problem solved? We are going to get a bit sophisticated in a moment but for now let's just apply what we have learned so far. Even the bog standard dinosaur salesperson of yore could make a better fist of this.

"Can it do calculations?"

"Is doing calculations important to you?" (The check back.)

"We have a big payroll each week."

"What have you been using to calculate that up until now?" (Talk about the past.)

"We employ 500 people all with different hourly wage rates."

"Wow, that's some calculation. Does that always go smoothly?" (Sympathize and dig deeper.)

Here I go again, simple to understand, basic stuff, but apply this thinking to every conversation and the world will be your lobster as they say! A new complication arises when we are dealing with expensive 'solutions'. Expensive solutions can only be worth buying for expensive problems. Therefore we must never make it look too easy. We need to grow the problem.

There is a classic bit of problem growing on TV at the moment, and I believe the campaign is promoting travel insurance. Maybe for a cheap break of just a couple of hundred pounds, spending another thirty percent or so of that on insurance is a bit of a waste of time – after all you aren't exactly going anywhere weird. The advertisement shows a cheery but vacuous check-in girl, who meets our cheery customer with the usual questions.

"Did you pack your bags yourself?" "Yes."

"Is there anything sharp in your hand luggage?" "No."

"Do you have travel insurance?" "No."

"Is one of your relatives a qualified doctor?" "No."

"Do you have a recognized qualification in international law?"

"Would your parents remortgage their home to charter a medically equipped jet aircraft?"

The value of the solution is increased by the cost of the problem.

They'll Beat a Path to Your Door

"We have got a rat somewhere."

"Let me show you the Acme Trap."

"How much?"

"£100."

"HOW MUCH?!"

Or,

"We have got a rat somewhere."

"How horrible, the words Bubonic plague spring to mind!"

The waters are going to muddy a bit here but there is something we need to sort out. There was a technique used by the early high pressure folk to terrify the customer with lurid tales (which, judging by the insurance adverts, does still have an effect). However, in large decisions particularly, the buyer can be quite sophisticated and resistant to such tactics. There is a ghastly old joke which asks, "What is the difference between a sprout and a bogey?" "The difference is that you can't get kids to eat sprouts!" The fact is, though, that you can get them to eat sprouts and you do it by giving them a packet of sprout seeds. If they grow the sprouts they will eat them. They will eat them for breakfast, lunch, and dinner, and it is the same with solutions to problems. If you said it, they don't believe it, but if they say it, it is the truth. This is true of all areas of persuasion, not just in these clever bits, so store that idea away in your 'must always do' file. Let's watch the rat thing again.

"We have got a rat somewhere."

"Really? Is that a problem?"

Our sales chums may claim that this is a 'Say No' question that could elicit an unwanted "No", but if the guy is a committed rat lover who is joyful about any potential infestation, a rat trap he will not buy! (My sales brain just slid into gear there. What about a humane trap that would catch them unharmed for petting and further study until they can be released back into the wild. Just a thought…)

Back in the real world…

"Yes it is a problem. I hate rats and one bit the head waiter and put him off work!"

"Off work, you say. It saves you paying him, I suppose! The rat did you a favour."

"Are you mad? It cost me double to get a useless agency replacement and the waiter is suing me for work related injuries."

"I doubt that happens very often, though, does it?"

"Nearly every week someone gets bitten."

"So if this guy earns £50 per day, that's £2500 per year on rat bites, but is that the only effect?"

"Apart from my horrified diners as the rats attack the staff."

"Sounds pretty awful. What have you tried so far to get rid of them?"

"Well, poison was a non starter. They just munched that with no effect. Then we had some idiot who was dressed like a clown with a flute, useless! I refused to pay him. Funnily enough I haven't seen my kids since, except the one with the IPod!"

"Let me get this straight. You have suffered financial loss, damage to staff morale, and lost customers. You have applied the usual solution to no avail. Therefore may I demonstrate the Acme Trap."

The Sword Swallower's Dilemma

You have turned suggested need into a genuine one. You have built the cost of the problem up so that your solution looks good value for money. Now it is time to demonstrate or offer your solution. It is time to put on a bit of a show! If I said, "I can balance a sword on my head", went ahead and did it, and then ambled off into the sunset, you probably wouldn't see much value in that. If you watch a circus performer who, let's face it, just balances a sword on their head, they put all this surrounding magic around it. The lights drop, the drum roll starts, a piercing spotlight picks out a sparkling figure who produces a sword that flashes wickedly in the lights. They slash at some fluttering tissue paper which is shredded into tagliatelle by the razor sharpness of the blade. You gasp, but not for the last time as our hero hoists this weapon's pointed end towards his forehead. The drum roll stops, everyone is holding their breath. Finally our hero whips his hand away from the precarious blade but too soon! It slips, and slices through the air, plunging deep in the floor, a millimetre from the performer's toes – another gasp! The audience sees a little trickle of blood on the performer's forehead but our hero persists. Is he trembling a little? Finally, he does it and we go wild. Put a little bit of that into your presentation.

"Well, is that the solution to my rat problem?"

"Getting rid of rats is never easy and I've got to say you have got one of the most dramatic infestations I have seen. So let's just see what the Acme Trap can do for you."

Thwack! Squeak! Silence!

"So if you could just OK the agreement, we can get the rest of the traps delivered!"

POINTS TO PONDER ON CHAPTER 15

1. Planning your journey of persuasion - who, what, why, where and how, are you going to persuade - is particularly important when making major decisions because inevitably there are going to be more people, more places, and more subjects involved than for a minor decision.

2. Don't get major and minor decisions confused. You will only end up doing more work than you need to or failing to get those big ticket sales.

3. Understand that the big decision could take a lot more time and effort.

4. Not making any decision can also be a decision. People can decide to do nothing -although not very helpful to us, it is still their decision which they may well make in response to our attentions, "No thank you, I will stay where I am."

5. The other person needs to be dissatisfied with their current position before they can adopt yours.

6. Talk about the past to learn about the future.

7. Be prepared to build the problem before you offer a solution.

8. Don't make it look too easy - put on a show.

CHAPTER 16

MEASURING SUCCESS

In which we discover how, in a small decision, a simple "Yes" is all we need for success, but in more complicated decisions it is very hard to know exactly where we are

A ll through this journey together the analogy of the map pops up, because on any expedition, if you don't know where you are, you are lost. In a major persuasion situation it is extremely difficult to know where you are. I love the Road Runner cartoons where the fanatical Wile E. Coyote pursues the Road Runner. In an interview, the cartoon's creator said that the coyote represented the perfect fanatic because he had been pursuing his quarry for so long that he had forgotten why he was doing it. This can happen to us. If our persuasion project goes on for too long we can sometimes forget why we are doing it and where we are. It is absolutely vital that we use the correct techniques to locate our exact position on the path between where we started and where we need to get to or we will just be tearing about lost in a desert, pursuing some mad chicken with absolutely no hope of success. What we need to know, therefore, is how we measure successful progress on our journey.

If you sell carrots and someone asks, "How much are your carrots?" you reply, "Two pence each", they then say, "Good! I will have one please." We could have a debrief and I would ask, "How is the carrot business? Successful?"

"I sold a carrot!"

"That's good, you were successful."

But if you say the subject did not buy a carrot, I could then say, "Then you have failed." Pretty cut and dried.

I Can See My House from Here

That is like very a short journey from, say, the refrigerator to the stove. You can see the destination from the starting point and you would have to be a bit dumb to get lost and end up at the dishwasher. On medium journeys, like from the fridge to the bedroom, it is familiar, well-trodden territory; you can usually see either the start or the finish rather than both at the same time, but you still know where you are. The problem is, with longer journeys on unknown routes, you get to a point where you can see neither start nor finish and in some cases you wouldn't actually recognize the finish if you got there. So how on earth do you know where you are, how far you have come and how far you have to go? With a major persuasion project, if we can't measure progress things start to drift alarmingly.

"How did you get on selling the multi-million pound road-building project to the Brazilians?"

"Great. They bought it and I have got the money in full!"

That is a success, so we can tick that one off.

"Awful. They threw me out and told me never to darken their door again."

That may be a failure – it could be saved, but all the clues point to a distinct lack of success. But what happens if things are less black and white...

"How did you get on selling the multi-million pound road-building project to the Brazilians?"

"Great! We showed them the models and plans and they were very impressed."

"So what happens now?"

"Well, they take our proposal, and the others, back to their Government who will let us know if we can take things further."

Don't get cross, but I think I might describe that as a failure. To go back to the journey, you have just got on someone else's bus with no idea of where it is planning to go, with the hope that it just might be going your way.

I Think I'd Describe That as a Failure

I have seen selling groups on major projects be in almost constant contact with the prospective client, with absolutely no positive outcome at all. **I think we must define a failure in a major decision to be when it just goes on and on but with no measurable progress towards where we want it to go.** What you can do for simplicity is treat each contact event as a micro carrot-sized sale. It is up to you to judge how big the carrot can be.

We have dealt at some length about qualifying and so on, and the conclusion must be that no meeting is a waste of time and no person you meet is useless. It is just that you must, by careful research and questioning, be precise about what is possible from this micro sale. The person can only give you what they are qualified to give you – the meeting is a way point on the clear route you have planned. Those engineers aren't qualified to order the motorway network but they can smooth the way for you to present to the Government minister concerned. Each of those mini sales will have a close, and the close must result in getting what that person is qualified to give you and that is *progress*. Rather than a close on each occasion, it is better to think of it as proposing an action. You should always come away with some action that you have proposed, even if it is only that next firm appointment to move things forward. If it is just you waiting for that "Don't call us, we'll call you", harsh though it may be you have probably failed. The prize may drift your way but you didn't achieve it by controlled persuasion which is what we are talking about here.

Out of Control

The successful structure of high level persuasion is all about control. Strangely, a lot of the steps are similar to the basic sale but there are subtle differences. It is sort of like living in one of those parallel universe movies where everything seems the same but really everything has changed.

From the 'dem' to 'objections' to 'closing the sale' we need to act differently.

When trying to get a big decision, the project we are proposing may be so huge and abstract that we don't even have a product to demonstrate as such. The classic solution is the presentation. When I worked in the bonkers world of advertising, the 'pitch', as it was called, had thousands spent on it, with the agency's top guns presenting ideas that were lavishly packaged with charts, film clips, and expensively constructed one-off samples.

Don't Upset The Tea Lady

I was called to a bank that was considering appointing a new advertising agency. The budget was many millions and I was asked by the board to sit in on the 'pitch' as an outside observer. We sat through a day of exotic and expensive presentations but one stood head and shoulders above the rest – they had clearly spent the most money but to good effect, and as the lights came up we were stunned by their sharp, slick approach. The CEO of the bank was a lord and came from the centuries-old family who founded the bank. "Well," he said. "I don't think there is much doubt over who wins our vote." At this point the door burst open and in came an elderly tea lady with her hair tied up in a head scarf, a cigarette dangling from her lips, nylon overall, and pushing a clattering trolley with tea and bickies. The lord addressed her with affection, "Well Aggie, what do you think of all this advertising business?"

She replied with a cough that showered his lordship with a fine coating of fag ash, "I didn't like that last lot!"

"Oh really, why not?" asked his lordship, apparently unconcerned by his patina of fine grey dust.

"They was really rude and off-hand with me and treated me like dirt they did!"

His lordship put his pen through their name on the list and we moved on to consider the second most elaborate presentation. The secret was that the lord had been the neglected child of the British ruling class, and Aggie had been like a surrogate mum to him. **Be very careful of who you dismiss as unimportant.** Treat everyone as if they and they alone, hold the key to your future prosperity. Fairy stories are always full of weird or repulsive people in need of modest help who turn out to be powerful fairies or witches, so watch your step!

Its All in The Presentation

As we prepare to persuade our subject, we may wish to produce a presentation of our own. What it will contain is a statement of how we understand our subject's situation, examples, plans and pictures of our own work or products, and a list of clients and unsolicited testimonials. If these vital tools are misused they are as good as useless. The presentation must follow a set three step plan. It's no good ambling into a client's office and saying, "I understand you've got rats. Here are some pictures of rats being slaughtered by the Acme Rat Killer. The Hotel Posh uses our traps all the time and I've got a letter from them somewhere saying that we are brilliant!"

The three steps give you solid control and build interest, commitment, and confidence.

Step 1

The presentation is put together as a whole presentation with pictures, graphs and statements, but there is one simple goal and that is to state and understand the size and value of the subject's problem (you can use your notes to good effect here. No notes? Shame on you.)

"Mr Nibbles, you have agreed a rat problem exists and you have tried the following solutions with limited success. The Hotel Posh, have you heard of them?" He should have done, it is his most famous and respected competitor but wait for the answer, "Yes." "Well, they had a very similar problem." Then list the aspects of the problem. Acknowledge the similarities and differences with the subject's problem.

Step 2

Put away the first presentation and reveal the second. "This is the solution that we put together for them". This part must be restricted to a detailed presentation of the solution or programme that you put together. Really put on a show Demonstrate the product, use video clips or pictures but be disciplined. This is the second part of the trilogy – don't give the game away.

Step 3

Put everything away and reveal part three, the outcome. "Within a week, there was absolutely no sign of any rodent activity, staff injury claims disappeared, and customer terror was significantly reduced." Of course, that is now exactly what your subject was expecting from the two preceding presentations, but the clincher is the unexpected benefits the project produced that your subject will clearly be able to translate into their own business. "But what was unexpected was, because the staff were being bitten less often, staff retention improved to the point that the induction training costs were slashed, making a saving of £400,000! Customer numbers surged to give a profit increase of nearly 80%. And what no one realized was that the rats had been gnawing through cables so then the incidence of fires and computer failure was completely stopped."

I may have said, put on a show, but what you have here is an irresistible drama in three acts with a happy ending.

More Than a Bit Concerned

While the longer decision process seems to mirror the shorter persuasion path, there are some subtle (and not so subtle) differences. In the final stages, for instance, we are ready to expect objections and now we know how to deal with them, but in a major decision process, because of the commitment required from both sides, a relationship of respect and trust must be built up with the subject. Without that, our job becomes impossible, but if you have mutual respect and trust, it is a bit tricky to see the other side as an adversary, victim, or prey. The word that springs to mind is 'partner'; as the process nears its conclusion, both sides have invested so much time, effort and resources that losing the deal would hurt everyone. It is unlikely, then, that objections in the normal sense will appear. Their comments may sound like objections to the untrained ear, but if we can see the other side as a partner we will understand that we are not hearing objections but concerns.

"We can't go ahead until we have dealt with this reliability issue."

In selling a food mixer or something, you would be right to say, "Before we deal with that, can I ask you – is this exactly the food mixer you were looking for?" When you get a 'yes' you can go on to describe the money-back guarantee that will deal with any reliability issues they may have, "doesn't it?" But if you are selling an atomic power station or an airliner this may be a little more than buyer resistance. Sure, by careful questioning check that this is the only issue, but most of all understand that your partner has a genuine concern. Get them to explain exactly what they mean and how they feel. Ask them what solution they would like and even if, to you, the concern is minor and easily solved, take it seriously and act professionally. Dismissing a concern can be fatal. Put on that show!

Returning to the classic path, after the objections we close the sale, but as we have seen the major sale requires a number of steps or micro-sales. Do you remember on our journey to Alaska, we met the local whose knowledge only stretched to the border of his village? We will meet people all along the way who have certain limits to what they can do for us, but we will find that we are limited also by our situation. The trick is to request and get the maximum possible, but no more, in that place with that person and at that time.

Planning an Ambush

Before I show you how, I suppose I ought to talk about place and time. I often tell my audiences to avoid getting ambushed. What I mean, on the simplest level, is that possibly you have the dreary job of door-to-door canvassing and selling some commercial consumable around industrial estates. Each place you meet the inevitable 'NO SALES-PEOPLE WITHOUT AN APPOINTMENT' but still you call at reception, accept the rejection, and leave a leaflet and your card. As ordered, you fruitlessly ask to see the buyer and then trudge on with your huge bag of samples and brochures. Then out of the blue some bored receptionist says, "Oh, our buyer, Mr Jenkins, says he can spare you a few minutes. Take a seat in reception and he will be out to see you."

A few minutes later, this man explodes through a door, tapping his watch with one finger and saying, "Come on, come on, I haven't got all day. I've got a meeting to go to. What have you got to show me?"

This is where it all falls to bits as you leap up, scattering papers and leaflets in all directions as you start to blurt out your sales pitch. He takes a leaflet and leaves with, "Don't call us, we'll call you" or something similar. I have seen a sale attempted across the roof of a car in a car park. Even if you have bribed your subject with a lavish dinner, golf day, or helicopter flight, none of these are the places to conduct a complete persuasion programme. Try, "It is very kind of you to see me, Mr Jenkins. I can see you are in a rush so can I just take this opportunity to arrange a more convenient time? Do you have your diary to hand?"

Perhaps if you have the bottle you could try, "Is there anywhere quieter we can go to discuss this, do you think?" and then if the time thing comes up, you could make a proper appointment.

The key is to get the maximum you can from the well-investigated situation that you see. Use a poor environment opportunity to simply take you to a better environment A poor time to take you to a better time. And with a person, the 'close' is, in this case, to get the most action they are qualified to give.

A great way is to run through that written checklist, pick out the points of agreement, and remind the subject of them. (It would be stupid to remind them of the disagreements.) Then propose the most action they are qualified to take. "So Chef Watkins, you felt the kitchen would run more smoothly with no rats, you agree that poisons have no place in your kitchen, you felt the Acme was well engineered and did a great job, your team found it easy to use, so may I propose that we meet again with you and the hotel manager at our works, where we can have lunch together and take matters further. Would next week or the week after be best?"

POINTS TO PONDER ON CHAPTER 16

1. You are only successful if you are making measurable progress.

2. Be careful who you upset. Everybody is important in the decision-making process, from the chief executive to the tea lady.

3. Plan your presentations meticulously and use the three step programme.

4. Don't get ambushed. Choose your battleground carefully.

5. Once the subject becomes your partner, their objections become concerns.

6. It is very much more difficult to measure success in a big decision than it is in a small decision.

CHAPTER 17

IT'S A REAL BARGAIN

In which we discover the to and fro, the cut and thrust, and the pure fun that is bargaining

On our journey of persuasion we have set off with the correct equipment and our destination in mind. We have encountered landmarks that have guided us and obstacles that we have learned to avoid. We may believe that now, finally, our destination is in sight with the commitment of our subject to proceed or to be convinced by our subtle wiles. The problem here is that this is where some truly weird games are to be played out. This is the time for bargaining and negotiation and it is also where all can be lost.

Let me show a very simple example of buying a cheap car and then we can get on to world politics and the settlement of bloody international wars – which, strangely enough, both require the same skill sets and guile.

As I have mentioned before, one of the buying signals we should look out for is if the subject starts becoming tricky, surly, or even aggressive. I said before, nice people don't buy, but what I might not have mentioned is why people do this. The explanation, weirdly enough, is that with certain reservations they have decided they want the deal. For the persuader this makes them outrageously dangerous.

Cheap at Half The Price

A huge amount of buying decisions are not made at the time of one-on-one persuasion. The cheap car is a prime example. Maybe you had a cheery non-threatening test drive; you said that you love the car but needed to "think it over". You toddle off with the brochures, price lists, and a vague valuation on your trade-in. The 'salesperson' (I put the title in quotes because they probably couldn't sell their way out of a paper bag) has lost control of you and the process and now can only wait for the capricious tide of luck to wash you back in. At home you peruse the brochures, check the finances, and compare the competing vehicles' specifications. From a subject's point of view, this is the right thing to do to avoid becoming the skilful persuader's plaything. Finally, after much thought, you make the decision to buy. You can afford it, they have plenty of the colours you want, and because of the economic climate they are desperate to sell. The mantra you chant to yourself is, "It's a buyer's market." The problem for the persuader, strangely enough, is that the subject, at this juncture, is starting to hold all the cards or, which is worse, they believe they hold all the cards.

The truth is that most decisions are made away from the hot fires of the persuasion process. The decision to marry, to go to war, or to buy fish and chips is all made elsewhere. Now we have our decision that we would be prepared to own this car or whatever, this is the time to drive a bargain. If our acting skills are up to it, we can seem unconvinced and disinterested, driving the other party to offer us ever more tempting delicacies of discounts, extras, and freebies to draw us into the deal. The dilemma for the persuader is that they don't know what cards the subject holds. Therefore we must, at a simple level, learn bargaining skills, and at a higher level, negotiating would be handy.

Call Their Bluff

Before all this starts, if you have got the bottle, you can remember that you are the pro and the subject may not be, so a bit of gentle exposing can be tried by the proficient operator.

"Hello again, how can I help?"

"Nothing really, I thought as I've got some time to kill, I might take another look at that little Thunderbolt 4000 you have in the showroom!"

"Oh, the Thunderbolt. If only you had come in earlier! I think my colleague has sold that one – at that price it was never going to be here very long."

And then, watch their face. I can feel another fidget of discomfort from you all. Yep, that is bare-faced trickery and I might feel uncomfortable but bear in mind the customer wasn't exactly being honest either. It also illustrates a very powerful message about the psychology of persuasion. **We always desire things we can't have.** I bet you want that Thunderbolt now the 'Sold' sticker is being pasted up. Actually, you think you deserve it more than the other guy. Tell you what, if we can hurry this paperwork through you could still have it!

Skilful Bargaining

Getting sensible for a moment, classic simple bargaining has some very simple but honest concepts and rules. The idea is that both parties are well-meaning and honest and would like to get a good benefit for themselves. Imagine that you are a genuinely honest used car dealer (hard to believe, I know, but a bit of fantasy role-play never goes amiss). The way your business works is that you pay fair market price for used cars. What reduces the price for you is that the sellers avoid risk and trouble, so for instance you buy trade-ins from the big dealers who just want to unload the cheaper stock; you may also buy from auctions where prices are low because the cars are uninspected, or from private sellers who want quick cash-without-responsibility or the hassle of a private sale. You inspect, service, and guarantee this car and put it up for sale at a reasonable mark-up which, over the years, give you a modest but sufficient salary.

Someone is looking for a safe reliable car for their daughter. If they spot the perfect car and you feel that there is no better first car but in the end you can't crack a deal, the customer leaves without the perfect car and you make no profit – you both lose. If you exploit their naivety and sell them a 6 litre V8 for three times what you paid for it, you win and they lose, but in the end you lose because that tactic is the death of repeat business and of course bad news travels fast. If the customer hears you are in deep financial trouble and that you need to shift stock fast to pay rent, they could knock you down to below your buying price – they win, you lose.

What we want is for the daughter to drive away thrilled and delighted with her pretty, bright, and reliable first car, and for us to bank a modest profit. In this case we both win.

The Win–Win Cliché

My criticism of this is that 'win–win' has become a truly ghastly cliché. Are you married? How long for? Who is winning? Stupid question because winning is never a word you would use to describe the progress of a marriage. You can have a mutually profitable and rewarding relationship with another person where 'win' is not even a term of measurement, but for now let's search for a good win–win.

Playing The Game

Firstly you must be well prepared. Most people aren't. Imagine that you have been promoting your enterprise to some minion who actually doesn't like or respect you that much. Not your fault, just one of those disappointed people that you find in mediocre bits of some businesses. The thing is that his boss has seen your offer, thinks the price is fair, and has told misery guts to call you in and do the deal. Now the problem for you is that you know nothing of this and this person is a game-player, and here is his game!

Knock! Knock!

"Come in!"

"Oh," you say, "I got your call that you wanted to see me."

"Did I? What about?"

"The last time I was here, we discussed our industrial food mixer."

"Oh yes, I remember. A bit pricey as I recall. Remind me how much it was."

"Well, it depends on the options."

"What options?"

"Well, there's the dough-hook and egg beater…"

"Look, I haven't got all day. Come on, some sort of ball-park figure will do."

"Well with the most popular options and extras, about £20,000."

"Phew! That much? My boss won't buy that."

"We sent you a quotation with a breakdown of all the costs."

"Did you?"

With this, there will be a theatrical rummaging amongst piles of papers and files.

"I tend to only hang on to the important stuff. Look, I like you, and I've got a lot of influence here. I think I could possibly twist the boss's arm into giving you a try – give me that price again and we will see if we can sharpen your pencil. If we can get near to a 20% discount I may even get you an order today."

The thing is, he is in a 'win–win–win' situation. He can deal with you at the price his boss expects – this is his fall-back position and still earns him brownie points – he could, on top of that, get even more discount which gets him an even bigger pat on the head from his lord and master. Best of all, he can make you unhappy which will make his day.

Prepared for Trouble

The answer to dealing with this person is impeccable preparation. You must marshal your facts, prices, costs and options, and all in hard copy. If you arrive with two slim files under your arm, one copy for you and one for him, when he tries the 'remind me' strategy, you can draw his attention to the short agenda in his copy file that confirms the reason for the visit that was agreed in his phone call. You can then draw attention to the copies of the quotations sent and the agreed points in other meetings. Be warned, this is not a stick to beat him with; if your meticulous preparation causes a humiliating climb-down you will have made an enemy for life. So your notes should be full of acknowledgement of his skill as a negotiator in other meetings.

"The last time we met, you were able to drive our prices down to our very lowest, but you also pointed out that the machine would be required for the autumn rush. As things stand, time is very tight for delivery in the time you specified in the letter you wrote two weeks ago, of which there is a copy in your file." You must have up your sleeve a small concession or reward so this guy can save face because, make no mistake about it, your meticulous preparation has got him nailed. Even congratulating him on being the toughest and most shrewd negotiator you have ever met will not go amiss. This preparation thing is very important in every deal that we do. As normal mere mortals we tend to always try and wing it.

The Truth Always Hurts

Let's get back to buying a car for a moment. We sail into a showroom and try to do a deal by making things up or using unreliable memory.

"Ah, but Bert's Garage offered free servicing."

"Really? Did that include the discount we are offering and which services does it include because the first minor service is free anyway."

If you go to buy a car, a house, or negotiate a repair with a neighbour, or a bit of building work with a contractor, just see how the situation changes if the slim file appears.

"OK, here is the deal that Bert's Garage has put in writing for me. I have included a print-out from a price comparison website that illustrates the type of prices on offer. And I have jotted down my options and costs if we fail to reach agreement today."

As a customer you would be a real pain – you can't lie because it is all there in black and white, but you will get the best possible fair deal. Benefit with honour, who could want for more. So before piling in, do your homework first.

Where Do They Stand?

We then need to find out where they stand on things. Before we move on together we have to understand that we are still in the territory of bargaining. There is a very simple concept that first you must ascertain the other person's position, then you state your position, and then the bargaining process helps you both to find a middle position that is acceptable to both parties. That is the way we will go for now but in true negotiating, that can be very dangerous. Just a thought for now, if you reveal your position, maybe the other person will give a big sigh of relief because they were prepared to give more than you have asked for. Hey, tell you what, to insure against that, exaggerate what you want! That's how strikes, wars, and divorces are caused, but more of that later.

Hidden Signals

So careful questioning will get them to state their position, and what, for now, they are prepared to offer. We need to make our position clear by stating our position, expectation, and options.

Propose offers and solutions, and watch for the other side's reactions. 'No' doesn't have to mean 'no'. People rarely just say the word "No" (actually you could try that, I bet it is very unsettling), what they do, even if quite aggressive, is to show little chinks in their armour, twinkles of light, signals that they are prepared to move. What we have to do is not see the rebuff but to see the hidden signals for compromise.

"No way! We would never deal at those prices. You must be joking."

Pretty final, then, but look again. "'At those prices?' At which price would you deal?" "So what you are really saying is that the price is the only thing stopping this deal?"

Look for, "In the current climate we couldn't...", "The way things stand...", "It's not in my budget...". Those are signals that tell us that there is an opportunity to change and make offers.

The final step is to make those offers but they must always be provisional and withdrawable. Elsewhere in this book we make very good use of that handy tool 'if' and 'then'. This is the time to use 'if' for all your worth.

"If we do increase our offer, then do we have exclusive rights?"

"We can't offer exclusive rights."

"Then we cannot really see the value in increasing our spend. Let's look at another angle to solve this."

If you say, "OK, we could pay more, but we are looking for exclusive rights", it looks the same but it really isn't. The other side hears two separate statements: "We can pay more." Yippee! "We want exclusive rights." "You're not getting 'em", but what they don't see is, "we've got more money we can put on the table but in return what else can we squeeze out of you?" 'If' and 'then' every time.

POINTS TO PONDER ON CHAPTER 17

1. Decisions are not always made in your presence - they can be made elsewhere.

2. A subject who appears to have made their decision can be very dangerous because now they want to bargain.

3. Unless you are a mind-reader you must be meticulous about preparing your options.

4. As you bargain, never make an offer that you can't comfortably withdraw using 'if' and 'then'.

5. It might appear like a refusal but it can often be a signal. Watch out for those signals and explore them.

CHAPTER **18**

EVERYTHING'S NEGOTIABLE

In which we learn that there is much more to negotiation than simple bargaining

As we climb towards the heady heights of negotiating skills, things start to change. The magic of good negotiating means that both parties can come away happy. It is like a sort of wonderful synergy where almost unbelievably everyone gets what they want. But it takes an extremely skilful negotiator to achieve this. Never fear, it is a skill that with practice anyone can master. And strangely enough, once again good old basic selling skills will help us.

My favourite story that has been oft repeated is the tale of two sisters fighting each other with screams and shouts and lots of hair pulling. You decide as a skilled negotiator that you should intercede. You discover that they are fighting over an orange. In the brilliant book on negotiating, *Getting to Yes,* the authors describe the two sides as wishing to divide a cake. Intuitively we start to divide the cake in percentage terms but the writers suggest that both sides could have everything they wanted (perhaps the whole cake) which seems impossible. You, as a fair minded person, must decide what to do about this punch-up and orange situation. Have a think; as a fair-minded reasonable person, what would be the correct thing to do? I usually get one of two replies. The diplomats thought you should offer to meticulously divide the orange in half , giving one half to each sister.

She Had Got Him Licked

I want to get on to dirty tricks later in this chapter but I can't resist this one because I have a kind of affection for people who won't play the game. I have a very pompous relative who has a very *not* pompous sister. Their mother despaired at the constant war over the fair division of the spoils. Cakes were often an issue and the last cake was a reason to go to war. The mother was given an elegant solution to outwit the kids. Tell one to divide the cake and the other can choose – a technique, I am sure, that can be applied to all division situations.

(There is a similar wage settlement scheme where the boss puts the offer and the workers put the claim in sealed envelopes, and the mediator awards to whichever is deemed the fairest with no compromise to the other party. When the envelopes are opened it is often the case that the figures are the same).

In the case of the siblings, the pompous brother got the job of dividing – which he did meticulously with dividers, a ruler, and other implements of accurate measurement. Without a single atom of difference between the two halves, the sister was allowed to choose. She picked up each half in turn, licked the icing on each, then said she didn't fancy either now that they had been "mucked about with" and left, leaving her brother apoplectic with rage – which was exactly the outcome she had wanted.

Neither Can Have It

The other option for the orange, I hear from the hawks amongst you, is to take the orange away so that neither of them can have it. This is a very dangerous option because, whilst it will unite these violent sisters, it unites them to want to attack you. So now you have acquired an enemy you didn't have before, a situation that peacemaking nations have discovered to their cost time and time again.

My father, a fluent Russian speaker, used to quote a dour Russian proverb on this subject which, roughly translated, stated, "When the squires agree, the peasant gets his arse kicked!" Therefore the peaceful option seems to be to give these sisters half of the orange each, but in this story that is when things get a bit strange. The first sister says, "Oh yummy, an orange", throws the peel away and eats the flesh. The second sister says, "Oh good! I can make my cake now." She grates the peel and throws the flesh away.

We could have given each side 100% of what they wanted but instead we allowed our prejudices and preconceptions to blind us to the solution. Go back to those cheesy old selling techniques and see the thoughts on 'benefits'. They didn't want the orange *per se,* they wanted its benefits. Remember, "Which means that...". The sisters wanted different benefits, "which means that I can eat the orange" and "which means that I can make that cake".

What we do in simple bargaining is, we UN-benefit things, and turn benefits into features – which of course is back to front.

They Just Want to be Happy

We want a successful profitable business. The workers want happiness, holidays, and a good family life. Those are benefits but instead of investigating them, we turn it into a fight over a feature which is money. While money is a sign of a successful company and money could make the workers happy, there are other ways of achieving that, and a dispute can be avoided with careful investigation of the divider option.

Fishing with Strawberries

Can I ask, do you like strawberries? You do? That's wonderful. How about a day's fishing? Knowing how much you enjoy strawberries I suggest that we bait the hook with a strawberry, but of course we know that a fish is more likely to be attracted to a worm. Again we are being guided by our prejudice because fish like all sorts of weird things from sweet corn to spam, but let's stick to worms for a bit. Another feature of a worm is, just because we wouldn't enjoy eating one, we ignore how much value our subject (the fish) would enjoy one.

What we always have to consider is the other party's interests, not the position that they are adopting. The truth is that positions are dangerous things. If we don't consider the other person's interest and just try to understand or change their position, we can find ourselves worse off. Negotiating contains a lot of the elements of selling in as much as we must make the proposition to our subject as attractive and as relevant to their situation as we possibly can – just as we do if we are trying to sell something. In fact, the persuasion skills in both negotiating and selling can be interchanged to great benefit.

They will Believe Their Own Words

Here is a quaint little stunt you can try. Get someone to pretend they are a customer of your lawn mowers or whatever you like. For this role play you want them to tell you that they have decided not to buy it.

"I have decided not to buy your lawn mower."

This is the clever bit; you now have a number of choices of how to react. The most obvious and natural is, "Why not?"

Bear in mind that this is a fantasy lawn mower, invented from thin air to satisfy some daft role play. The reaction is astonishing and you immediately start to generate a position in the other party.

"It's too expensive."

"Anything else?"

"It's not very well made."

"I haven't got a lawn!"

You never mentioned price, the mower doesn't actually exist so how can they attack the quality, and they do have a lawn. "Why not?" has forced them to create a position, justify it, and dig in. The fact that it was a fantasy lawn mower must demonstrate to us that, by probing a position with the question "Why not", the other party is provoked into inventing stuff. So when you get the genuine "I don't think we'll proceed", don't provoke things with "Why not", and if you already have, don't believe everything you then hear.

What can you do? You could try:

"I don't think we'll proceed."

"Oh, I am sorry to hear that. What would we need to do to get you back on board?"

Interestingly and usefully for us, we can reverse the process to create a position that favours us.

"We are considering using your company."

Again, resist the natural inclination which is to gallop about shouting, "Yippee! You won't regret this, we're brilliant" accompanied by a lot of hand-rubbing. Instead, ask, "Oh, I am pleased, why did you choose us?"

At the job interview:

"I am so pleased to be shortlisted for this job. What is it you saw in me that made you feel I could fill the role?"

They immediately start to invent reasons for their decision and, as they do, they become more convinced of their position. When you see two friends arguing over differently-held beliefs, get them to swap positions and argue each other's case – they soon convince themselves. Going against our own intuition and prejudice is essential. To a kid who is being bullied, the only thing worse than a sign on their back saying "Kick me" is one that says "Please don't kick me".

Nothing Personal

When people fly at you, finger wagging, raging, demanding, and accusing, you start to take it personally. Worse, you start to be annoyed and dislike the other person. The key word here is 'person' and if the word 'you' is used too often it becomes personal, when what we really need is to understand the other person's interests. We may find that the solution may cost us nothing if the other party's interests are understood. The fish wants the worm, we can't understand why it would, so if we employed fish they may demand money that we haven't got and they could go on strike, crippling our bicycle-testing company simply so that they could go out and buy worms. Finally after many trying weeks, we change our position and offer half the money that the fish are asking for. They can't hold out much longer and grudgingly accept and return to work with a mutinous and belligerent attitude. With their pay rise, they go and purchase worms from the man we have paid to deal with our plague of worms.

Feelings

We must, through careful questioning, identify the subject's interest. We must stay calm and not get emotionally involved. If you feel that their behaviour is totally out of control you can express how you feel, but never never use "you" as in "you liar", "you let me down", "you are really annoying".

Just express your genuine feelings:

"I feel I'm not getting all the facts."

"I feel disappointed."

"I feel quite upset."

They can interpret for themselves the cause of your feelings without you provoking them into justifying a hard position with the "you, you" stuff.

War is a Serious Business

Let's go back to the sisters with the orange for a moment. The argument over the orange may seem petty but when it comes to wars things get a bit more serious. If you remember, one solution was to divide the orange fairly into two halves. If we look at Korea or Vietnam, the dividing ended up with years of conflict. Taking the orange away from both of them was how the British tried to pacify Northern Ireland – all that ended up with was the British being attacked. However, after the war between Israel and Egypt, there was an argument over the occupied desert. Dividing it could have been an option but instead both parties' interests were carefully explored. It turns out that Israel had no desire to own a desert, they just felt very uncomfortable with Egyptian tanks on their border and they felt a few hundred miles of desert offered a fine buffer zone. The Egyptians were very keen on the ownership of the desert and felt it their homeland. The answer was to demilitarize the desert and let the Egyptians have it back, thus giving both sides everything that they wanted.

Go Looking for Trouble

A negotiation must be taken at your pace, don't let the other party provoke an emotional reaction, and you should use careful questioning about their interests. As we have seen throughout this book, questions are the most powerful tool we have, but when negotiating, the questioning should be done with even more flair and dexterity. When you get your answers, don't react immediately but delve deeper. Don't be too keen to wind things up even if you feel that more questions could lead to even more trouble. If you want to hang off a cliff with a rope, test it with sand bags three times your weight in the privacy of your own home If it breaks, that may be disappointing and trying, but not half as trying or disappointing as plunging screaming thousands of feet into a yawning abyss with your arms flailing wildly. So don't be afraid to test the agreement.

"So, rather than extra money and longer hours, if we can always provide you with as many worms as you want, you will be happy?"

"The odd maggot might be nice."

Don't be tempted to be too hasty with, "Well I'm sure a few maggots won't be a problem."

Remember to understand how important and valuable something may be to the other party even if it isn't to you. While it may be cheap and easy to provide maggots, firstly you threw away a bargaining chip and secondly you devalued and thereby insulted the other party's claim. Remember, put on a show and "if" and "then".

"Phew, maggots. I wasn't expecting that one. You drive a hard bargain, Mr Trout. Let's see where we are. My understanding is that if we could include a few maggots in our worm offer, then you and your fellow shoal would return to cycle testing for us."

Don't Get Personal

I was tempted to put, "Our very generous worm offer…" but that is fatal. Never describe yourself or your opinions on your offer in glowing or exaggerated ways – there is no better way to wind the other side up.

"Well, I think we have been very fair with you."

"I am surprised you have rejected this generous offer."

If you really want trouble, try holding your lapels as you tell your subject how kind, generous, and reasonable you are while, by implication, you suggest how pig-headed, unreasonable and dishonest they are being.

Just as in selling, run through the key points and test them, all the time using questions as your tool of choice. Even if the other party is aggressive or unreasonable you are more likely to defuse that by questions.

"How do you feel that waving that axe around will progress this negotiation?"

Even if you have a useful point to make, express it as a question.

"May I make a suggestion?"

Don't then just plunge into the suggestion, but use the mighty power of silence to give you a forceful opportunity to put your point across in a patch of calm that will allow you to be listened to.

Indecent Exposure

Preparation again is the key to success as long as success is getting an acceptable fair outcome. The truth is that if we are unprepared we have a tendency to be dishonest. I hear you gasp with indignation, but if someone asks you whether you could afford more, or could buy cheaper elsewhere, or if that was your best price, if you don't actually know those answers, you tend to make them up – and worse than that, to invent them to favour or support our position. Well, you can rest assured the other side are doing the same. Before we remove the splinter (or plank) from our own eye, let's see how we may have to get a bit tough with our subject. A word of warning here, use your judgement. If a person who wants to do business with you is using dirty tricks and you don't really need a relationship with them, then you can get a bit tough. This is not aggressive or unkind, but if people are not honest then they will feel sore if they are exposed. So be warned! DON'T TRUST ANYBODY.

OK, end of health warning. This is what you do. You remove the whole concept of trust out of the process and only base your decision on facts. There is absolutely no use for trust in a positive or negative way. All statements have to be proved and tested.

"This car has had just one careful owner."

"That's marvellous. If you could give me that owner's name and phone number I can certify the history of the car."

"What's the matter, don't you trust me?"

"I hadn't considered trust one way or the other. I just want to purchase a solid reliable car."

Hidden in The Small Print

I have just been stuffed by a travel insurance company. When I tried to claim for a cancelled trip because of the collapse of my mother-in-law, who wasn't travelling but couldn't be left, they pointed to Clause 44B or whatever, that stated at the time of the purchase of the policy they should be made aware of all friends or relatives who may fall ill and which might prevent travel, and as my mother-in-law was in her late 80s, she could be considered a risk. How many of you have elderly relatives? Would you cancel your holiday for your granny's funeral? Well, you had better tell your travel insurance company. However, when purchasing such a product you may well draw attention to weird conditions and sub-clauses. The other party, if less than honest, will attempt to brush them off.

"Oh, the elderly relative clause? That is really only there as a technical point. We would never enforce it."

"Really, then remove it before I sign."

That is just me being grumpy about some cheap travel insurance, but it isn't so funny when purchasing a house or signing an investment agreement. Do your homework and then face to face unblinkingly ask for any unreasonable conditions to be removed. If it becomes a deal breaker, are you sure it is a deal that you want.

"Mm, mortal soul, hey? Sign in blood, hey? Riches for life? How long is life? Why in blood? How about a no obligation trial period?"

Poor old Faust would still be with us!

How Low will You Go?

It is time now to look at our own preparation and honesty. Without preparation we cannot help but be dishonest. How much do you want for your car? £5000? Why that figure? Because you may think that is what it is worth?

Let's imagine that you are a bit desperate for cash and you have to sell the car. What is the least you would take for it? Have a think. I've got all the time in the world but remember you've got to sell and I won't be mucked about. Oh, you've got a bottom figure in mind but you won't tell me? Maybe for a quick sale you have a minimum figure of £4000, and that is the very absolute minimum you would take. OK, let me see how much money I have. Well nearly there, I have £3999.99 – 1p short. Well of course you would take that, but then £4000 wasn't your actual bottom line – you weren't being honest. I know, just a penny, but hold on a minute, I've only got £3999.00. Of course you would take that, it is only a pound.

I was putting this idea to a group of business people and Mr Grumpy said, "If you start tricks like that, I would walk away and you would never get the car. I would rather burn it." From his point of view, that's just stupid because he has no car and no money, but it should also be a warning to us that there are some people who would rather blow up than give in.

Kill The Wabbit!

I often challenge my intellect and get my inspiration through the medium of cinema, and I remember a situation where Bugs Bunny and Yosemite Sam are on the deck of a ship full of gunpowder. Bugs would throw a lighted match into the gunpowder and then just smile. Yosemite Sam would always try to out-wait him but his nerve would break and he would run below to extinguish the match. Watch out for the Bugs Bunnys of this world. Even if you can get what you want, you must save their face before they blow you both up.

Develop Your Backstop

What we have to develop is a backstop, a truthful backstop. What we need to do is to go out and get the car professionally valued. Perhaps someone would offer £3750. This is less than we expected and they would be getting a bit of a bargain, but in exchange we can ask for that offer in writing. When that written offer is put on the table, we have proof that we have a firm offer that is currently being refused.

What you want is to exchange your car for cash. You have demonstrated in writing that you have other offers – cash for the car. Then don't start to dilute your argument of value for money cash, for carpy wingy minor points that dilute your key objection.

"If I sell it now, I'll have to walk home."

"If I take less, my friends will say I'm stupid."

"That won't leave me any money to go to the pub."

Piling on the reasons doesn't strengthen your argument, it waters it down, and the other party will pick just one argument – usually the weakest – to shake your resolve.

"Listen, if this is about financing your drinking…"

Let Them Blow Off Steam

As you will have noticed, in simple bargaining there is quite a bit of toing and froing, but this is less the case in negotiating. A well-prepared supported case with a backstop in writing should result in a satisfactory outcome. The other party could well not enjoy this process because, beforehand, they were probably preparing all sorts of jolly tricks and wheezes. Through preparation, to be frank, you have outwitted them. The state of feeling outwitted is not a comfortable one and we have to deal sensitively with their negative emotions and even dirty tricks. If they respond with anger, allow them to let off steam but make no comment. Ask them questions and then shut up and listen with understanding, however outrageous they are being. Try asking for their advice as to how to get over their upset and accusations.

"If you were me, what would you do to put this right?"

If they are really up to no good, gently exposing it puts an end to that one.

"I don't think you want me to credit check this because you know there is outstanding finance."

Too Much Invested to Walk Away

A final thought on negotiating, which I suppose also applies to persuasion, is a bit of a weird one. You would think, if things dragged on in a tedious and repetitive way, ping ponging back and forth, that it would antagonize the other party. One of the finest books on negotiating warns about 'ping pong' negotiating, but – and it is a strong but – picture yourself trying to purchase an expensive item. You have visited the salesperson a few times. Each time they have moved a bit more, you have taken the demonstrator for a day. The Sales Manager has got involved; you go back for a third or fourth visit. In your mind you have gathered strong argument and a final offer. Another small movement occurs, you have another demonstration, top buttons are loosened, a third cup of coffee is drunk, it is getting dusk, you hear the car tyres outside splashing through the puddles, people are hurrying home for a hot supper and finally the salesperson pushes back their chair, snaps their pencil, wipes the sweat from their brow and says, "That is it! I am done. We cannot do another thing."

This is not exactly the deal you want, but you have made a huge investment in time and effort on this particular path. If you walk away and start again, all that thought, time and emotion has been wasted and you are back to square one. The conclusion is, therefore, that against all received wisdom you can wear someone down!

POINTS TO PONDER ON CHAPTER 18

1. Always investigate the other party's interests before dividing the spoils and never assume you know what they want.

2. Whilst negotiating, you need to get people to justify why they do want to work with you, not why they don't. Ask the wrong questions and they will soon invent reasons why they hate you.

3. It's the deal that you want so don't let things get personal.

4. You can express your feelings as long as you don't blame them or try and guess their feelings.

5. Don't be too hasty to reach agreement. Always test things carefully.

6. It's never about trust. If anyone asks you to trust them they probably shouldn't be trusted. The small print is there to catch you out, and if they won't remove it, it's probably a deal you didn't want.

7. Make sure you develop a firm backstop or you will always be pushed lower than you wanted to go.

CHAPTER 19

PERSUASIVE MARKETING

In which we find the subjects for our persuasive talents and build their expectations

Before you skip this chapter believing that marketing is not relevant to you, bear in mind that we all have something to market. The persuasion techniques that you may have discovered in this book are completely useless if you have no one to persuade. You may have love to give – is putting your details in a lonely hearts column, marketing? I think it is. When you send your CV off for that job, surely that is marketing too. Creating these expectations for our subject simply gives us the opportunity to persuade. If you have a small business you may call the subjects "customers" and marketing helps you to find them. If you are in direct sales, you would call them "prospects" – but you still have to find them. Or, if you are just lonely, you might like to think of them as "friends", but you still have to track them down. In all these cases, the classic skills of marketing (I can think of no other name for it) are what we need to learn.

I make my living by public speaking; my presentations are planned to inspire crowds of eager business leaders (and not so eager employees) to ever greater heights of understanding and achievement. The most fatal flaw a presenter can have is to be boring so my business points are put across with a lot of gambolling, shouting, stories and exaggeration. When talking about marketing I create the fiction that most people in marketing are named either Jervais or Tarquin and are not entirely in touch with the real world.

The story continues with a chain of roadside diners that is failing badly and feels that the solution could be a bit of marketing. A number of businesses work on a very naïve formula which, on the face of it, simply states that (i) the business is failing because not enough revenue is coming in to it, (ii) that finding and keeping customers is the only activity that can generate revenue, and therefore (iii) if they could simply find more customers, they will find more revenue. (What they fail to ask is, where did the original customers they had go to? Is their company too big and unwieldy for the limited amount of potential customers that there are? Are they making maximum profit from every customer they have?) But for now, their simple minds tell them that more revenue comes from more customers, marketing is the science that finds customers, so therefore they could do with a bit of marketing.

Could you do with a bit of marketing? Why?

A constant aim throughout this book is to give you unexpected power simply by making you conscious of why you are doing things. If you have a small business, perhaps a great fresh brochure would do the trick. What trick is that then? When you commission this thing, what are you expecting it to achieve for you as regards persuading people to do business with you?

I am not immune from this failure either. For ages I have worked with a great bunch of characters who built my website for me. Although a bit weird, they are brilliant and because they used to lurk in a cave-like office behind a bar, I christened them the Techno-trolls. I really like my website with its video clips and shop. The Techno-trolls regularly pop up with new ideas – one that broke the budget so we didn't use it involved a cartoon me walking to the front of the screen and chatting to the visitors. (But even without that it is all very jolly – come and see it sometime, www. geoffburch.com). But what does it do for me? Do you have a website? What does it do for you? What does it tell the world about you? Or does it not actually tell the world, but only the three people who bother to visit it Some people take 20 million hits, some the low tens. Why? Actually my website brings me most of my work and many of my sales but I don't know why, and I don't know how to make it work harder. Apart from it being a place for people to find me, I am not sure where it fits in my persuasion process, but I am working on it and think I can see some results. **The point is, before you do anything, ask yourself why you are doing it and how you are going to measure it.**

The Vital Ingredient

Continuing to use the journey route map to persuasion analogy, measurement is the next vital ingredient. However you travel measurement is, and always has been, a vital element. A thousand years ago, the weary footsore travel-ler was either encouraged or discouraged by the mileages written on stones and wooden signposts. Almost as soon as cars were invented, the speedometer and milometer were installed. A few hundred years ago, Britain's greatest cash prize was offered to the person who could invent a timepiece that could stay accurate on a ship. Why? Simply to accu-rately measure distance and find out exactly how far along the journey they had travelled. Every motorway and free-way sign gives destinations, along with that magic number, the mileage. So, in your planned and intentional interaction with other people, whether it is a sale, a romance or a career, you need to ask yourself where exactly you are, you need to know how far you have already come, and you need to appreciate how much further you need to go.

Not What They Expected

Back to our diner. Business, as I have said, is declining and they think marketing is the answer. It probably is but if they don't know why, there is trouble in store.

They go to meet Jervais and Tarquin and explain the situation. Actually, what they explain is the situation as they see it. Why are you reading this book? It would suggest from the title that reading it will help you to become more persuasive, but if it gives you that power how will it help you? Will it help you to get a first date with the person you desire? Will it make people become your customers? Can it make your current customers pay more and on time? Or could it make the people who work for you work harder and with greater loyalty? What our diner owners see is that their declining fortunes are a result of declining customer numbers. That is what they ask Jervais and Tarquin to address.

This is just their sort of territory and they leap into action.

"What you need," they cry as they scamper around their office, "is to promote yourselves. A promotion! The Autumn Promotion! We will do an autumn leaf-shaped voucher, suggesting that your prices are falling like autumn leaves, and every home in the country will have one and as long as they purchase one adult meal they will receive a further adult meal entirely free!" (This is called a 'Bogof', by the way, Buy One, Get One Free.)

Will this succeed? Imagine you own these diners. How will you tell if this 'promotion' has been a success?

One of the biggest business guru chestnuts is the story of the mogul who said, "Half our marketing budget is wasted, but the problem is, we don't know which half!" Ho ho, we chuckle, what a clever chap. I thought it was very funny and I chuckled appreciatively every time a big client said it as if they had just thought of it, until one day a very bright colleague said, "How do you know it's half?"

Stunned shuffly silence and a thunderbolt realization that we have no idea where we are.

Gangsters Can Do It

Marketing, sales, bribery, threats of violence, and chat up lines, if successful, do just one thing, and that is to give us an opportunity. To make this a bit clearer, let me take one of the more dubious techniques and that is the threat of violence.

Many years ago I had some business interests which involved having to trade with what I can only describe as east London gangsters. They were actually a funny, lively hard-working bunch led by a very close-knit family. Beneath the cheery cockney exterior, though, lay a mentality that matter-of-factly saw violence as part of their business tool kit. They would invite clients to give them a work contract and suggest with some evidence that the prospect's future health and safety would be better served by the granting of the contract. Judges often refer to mindless violence but in a way this was worse because it was intelligent, well-planned violence. I am not suggesting at this point that you don your brass knux or pick up a sandbag; this extreme example is to provoke you to think. This frightening approach was used to grant the family an opportunity. In actual fact, they were bright enough to then go on to give faultless service, at competitive prices, along with the understanding that the new client was now a 'friend' of the family and could expect to be free from unwanted attention from any lesser criminals. In other words, they exceeded expectations and delighted the customer. Lazy low life crooks who think that they can simply threaten and give nothing will finally provoke the victim into turning them in. When you look at successful crime syndicates they deliver the goods, whether it is clubs or casinos. Ask yourselves, why do they bother to make the premises smart and clean with well dressed and deferential staff? Because – and I will say it yet again – whatever method you use, marketing can only grant you an opportunity.

J The chat-up line gives the opportunity of a first date.

J The tray of coffee samples gives the opportunity of a first taste.

√ The office cleaner got me to give him an opportunity to meet a potential client.

√ The salesperson wins an opportunity to supply that first order.

The point is, if we are going to expend a great deal of time, effort and money on a marketing campaign, are we ready to recover the cost of that campaign from the customers who come in? I am always shocked and surprised when I talk to a roomful of salespeople who often have no idea what their company's marketing strategy is, have no knowledge at all of any special offers that have been widely promoted and, worst of all, have no connection with or confidence in the marketing strategy – which, after all, has only been set up to give them the opportunity to meet potential new customers. It is no good investing in any kind of marketing if everything else you do is not set up to recover that cost by securing profitable business from the activity.

Let Me Twist Your Arm

What about bribery? Often cheap and elegant but still just an opportunity. Just imagine that you are reading this book to help grow your small coffee shop and, just like our diner, you feel that a simple business boost would come from more customers. "Aha," you cry, seeing a section on marketing, "that's what we need!" But what sort of marketing? Let's start with a half page advert in the local paper. You do a tough deal with them and they give you a whole page for £400 (you'd be lucky! I think you could expect to pay thousands but hey ho).

The next day your small coffee shop has one hundred people in it. Twenty is too many at one time so there is trouble brewing anyway but, more to the point, they cost you four pounds each. They drink a cup of coffee, price two pounds, cost to you one pound, profit one pound, loss three pounds.

So let's try good old bribery. Go off to a public place and give away free coffee vouchers "Bring this voucher and get a free cup of coffee!" The benefit is that you can control the flow. Each person who ignores the bribe of the free coffee costs you virtually nothing, the ones who reclaim it cost you only a pound – half the loss of the advert and much more controllable. If the numbers overwhelm you, stop handing out the vouchers. So that's good then, a much slower way of losing money than straight advertising.

The Wandering Husband

It is time for another awful joke. A woman rushed up to a friend and said, "I hate to gossip but I thought that I had to tell you. I have just seen your husband chatting up the new pretty young barmaid!"

She appeared totally unconcerned and replied, "Oh, is he. I can't say I'm particularly bothered."

"Aren't you worried?"

"No, not really!"

"Why on earth not?"

"We had a dog once that used to chase cars but if he ever caught one he wouldn't have been able to drive it!"

If You Caught a Customer, Would You Know What to Do with Them?

Back to the office cleaner. What did he do with the opportunity?

The diner and its autumn leaf campaign. What if it had worked?

Your coffee shop? Do you see what we have done? You said that you needed customers, so quite simply we went out and bought you some. They cost a pound each. In marketing terms that is something of a bargain. In coffee shop terms it is a bit more edgy. So now you've got them, are you a bit like the dog and have no idea what to do with them?

First question is, how are you going to recover your pound? This is yet again grandmother and sucking eggs time, but let's for a moment consider profit. Profit is the difference between what it cost you and what you get. In the case of the coffee shop, it's wages, rent, coffee, and marketing costs. So now you have given the coffee away, how do you get that pound back? Either by inviting that customer to spend more on that visit, or by returning over and over again in the future to recover that initial outlay.

See You Next Fall

Seems simple, but back to the diner and the autumn leaf promotion.

You receive one of these leaves and decide to give it a try. You are met by an eighteen stone kid with a badge that states, "I'm Kevin and I'm here to help", wearing a bright red boiler suit that's so tight it's flossing his bottom. He brings, after a very long wait, a plate of tepid grey stuff and you ask, "What is this?" The cheery reply, "Dunno, never eat veg myself."

Eureka! It's his fault, isn't it? We are shovelling the customers in and he and his kind shovel them out again BUT...you know it isn't his fault, the fault is much more fundamental. While you make all these extravagant promises to your prospects, just make sure your products, offers, and everyone involved can deliver the promise. Market in as vigorously as you market out. It isn't just the people who work for us either. There is a famous saying that states, "when you are up to your arse in alligators, it is very hard to remember that you set out to drain a swamp". We ourselves often forget – or don't even realize – what expectations we have created. We cheerfully use power words like 'excellence, delight, and wow' without considering the fact that that is actually what our subject may expect. In other words, we must all understand the expectations that we have created to attract our subjects, and must be prepared to deliver or even exceed them if we want to see a return on that investment which we made. We can either profit on a single meeting with a customer, cheerfully knowing we are never going to see them again – which is classic high pressure selling – or we can get a return on this investment from repeat business which means making our subject happy and satisfied every single time we meet them – which is a big challenge.

Let's examine what our sales and marketing are going to do for us in the first footsteps on our journey of persuasion.

To persuade anyone, we must create an opportunity to persuade, but the other edge to this sword is that it also gives us an opportunity to disappoint.

Great Expectations

We get our opportunity by creating expectations. From the flashy adverts to the rock star who comes on stage with a cucumber in his trousers – the result could be a horrible disappointment in both cases.

Marketing people have taken issue with me over this rather simplistic view, saying that another of their tasks is brand awareness, but what if your brand is rubbish. There are a number of very well known companies, shops, airlines, and conglomerates who are famous alright – famous for being awful. Of course I wouldn't dare mention them here but if while on a walk with me I shouted "Dog turd" at you, previous experience, legend, and expectations would not make you want to jump in it. In fact its fame should hopefully get you to do just the opposite. Therefore, being a familiar name doesn't always help to persuade.

We persuade by creating expectations of wonderful things but we must be prepared to deliver. Second chances are difficult to get.

POINTS TO PONDER ON CHAPTER 19

1. Every business thinks that all they need are more customers. Marketing, sales and gangsters find them by making promises (or threats).

2. This will always have a cost that can only be recovered when that promise has been kept.

3. It is very easy to make big promises, it is very difficult to keep them ourselves, and even more difficult to get the people who work with us to keep them.

4. Rather than blame everyone else, make sure you market in to everyone involved, as well as out to your potential customers. In other words, make sure everyone involved understands, is able, and agrees, to keep the promises that you and your 'marketing' have been making.

5. Anyone can buy a customer but not everyone can profit from them.

PART FOUR

THE PSYCHOLOGY OF PERSUASION

CHAPTER 20: IT'S ALL IN THE MIND!

In which we learn that people make decisions in their heads.
When we understand how this process works we can
influence the outcome

CHAPTER 20

IT'S ALL IN THE MIND!

In which we learn that people make
their decisions in their heads. When we
understand how this process works we can
influence the outcome

As we come to the end of our persuasion journey, we need
to understand where this journey took place – and that
is in our head. When we meet our subject the processors
of their brain are saying, "No, not convinced". Our actions,
words, and planned interactions will waft them gently from
that original position to one of, "Yep, I am totally convinced".
Therefore, before you rush out and practise your finely-
honed persuasive art, perhaps a little understanding of the
psychology of persuasion may not go amiss.

We believe what we believe. We are sure the sun is a ball
of fiery atomic energy that our little rocky planet whirls
around. We know in the depths of the sea, so deep that we
can't go there, strange creatures lurk, and we know electricity works benignly but potentially dangerously in the wires
of our homes.

Really?

Have you been to the sun, or into the deep ocean? Have
you actually seen electricity? So why are you sure those

things are true? Simply because you have been convinced by persuasive argument. Just as you have been convinced of these things, be sure that you could be just as convinced of things that are not true.

We have Ways of Making You Believe

Propaganda has been a powerful form of persuasion throughout history. Though of course we are far more subtle now...

Really? Think of the way we are told that dairy products are bad for us, or that reality TV shows can broaden the mind.

For us, the lone persuader, what it can teach us is the power of emotive words and how to use them. What we can do is create pictures in the minds of the other parties, and the palette of colours we can use is our choice of words. Whilst oppressive regimes use the image of scurrying rats to portray the need to exterminate their enemies, we fall for the same tricks. We may not be bothered to hear that Jack Smith is the elected spokesperson of his colleagues, but we know just what sort of immoral, destructive person he is when he is called a 'trade union boss'; or Carol Brown, who might appear to be a financial auditor, but as a 'fat cat banker' she has brought us to the edge of destruction. For a large amount of the discussion about persuasion, we have seen it as a two handed game, but sometimes we need to persuade a crowd by 'rabble rousing' (golly, now I'm doing it), or perhaps we need to persuade in writing, or through some broadcast or recording medium. All we can do is guess what will appeal to the audience and then go for it. By picking our words carefully, using stories, anecdotes, and fables, we create a film show in the other person's head.

Facts, figures, and evidence – however irrefutable – will always lose our subject's attention if they are not spiced up with a few colourful, attention-getting anecdotes. If you like things to be a little more formal, set up your persuasive presentation like this. Tell your audience the concept.

"Fellow Postpersons! We should always be cautious of unknown dogs."

Tell the story in a technicolor way.

"I remember once I had a parcel to deliver and I thought it odd that anyone would have a one-metre high cat flap. I didn't have to wonder for long as this horror burst out like a bullet from a gun, the shredded remains of the milkman hanging from its drooling maw. The hound of the Baskervilles had nothing on this thing. If I hadn't hurdled 27 garden fences, a little like an Olympic gold medalist, I wouldn't be speaking to you today!"

Then finally give them something they can try for themselves.

"So when you are in a neighbourhood you don't know, ask if there is a dog loose, look for bones and blood stains, and rattle the gate from the safe side."

Vive La Difference

This is when we have gauged our audience but we also need to understand how different people's thought processes are constructed. If we can understand what makes someone tick, we can make them tick to our tune, as it were. If life was a play, then our subject would be the hero and the part we play would be the character that makes them feel best. Most normal people (and most people aren't normal) have a thing that the professors call the 'ego ideal'. This means the person that we would most like to be, kind, attractive, thoughtful, moral, respected, and admired. Immaturity can do awful things to our ego ideal, and when you see the spotty 17-year-old in the ankle length leather coat despite soaring summer temperatures, his ideal is the sinister dark stranger living off the grid, his eagle eyes flicking suspiciously across the faces of us unsuspecting cattle. He mixes compassion for us with a little contempt. Truth is, he is a prat, and if you go and tell him that with some maturity you will ruin his day, but we are here to persuade. More to the point, if we are trying to persuade, we must not overturn our subject's beliefs and prejudices. We may be able to prove our case, but we will make them feel bad and then they hate us for it.

For instance: "I'm not sure this grinder is safe. What if I poked my finger in it?" The cheery reply, "Who on earth would be stupid enough to poke their fingers in a grinder" will just serve to drag that person away from their ego ideal. Their concern has proved to you and the onlookers that they are not thoughtfully cautious, but that they are an idiot. True, but unproductive!

Preserve Their Pride

I often have quite heated discussions with people who feel that they have to prove their point; they must right the wrongs and crash the misconceptions. The trouble is, they are rotten persuaders. What could you have said?

"You are absolutely right. Few people are shrewd enough to be aware of the dangers of high powered machinery, and with that concern in mind our designers have fitted a safety lock-out unlike a lot of cheaper but less-safe designs."

You appreciate their perspicacity and their ego is rewarded and they are happy. They like being happy and will come back to you time and time again to be made to feel that way – even if they have to buy something every time they do.

Ideas Above Their Station

This is based on the normal ego, but a lot of senior people, usually men of short stature, have an ego that actually exceeds their ego ideal – they think they are right because they know they are right. They probably dress as Napoleon in the privacy of their own home. They see themselves as born leaders and the definition of a leader is someone who does all the talking and makes all the decisions. That gives us a bit of a dilemma because we need to impart new information and ideas to them whilst all the while encouraging them to think the whole thing was their idea. Believe it or not, they can actually swallow you saying, "That idea of yours to fit a finger-proof lock-out is inspired" even if it was never their idea. As you make your pitch or presentation be completely aware of the other person's feelings. Before you take these comments too literally, understand where these feelings come from. They are needs, as important as oxygen, water, and food. They support our lives just as surely, and without them we fade and die. Some psychologists describe them as drives, the drives that drive our whole being. Some claim we have thousands but most agree that there are eight basic ones. By understanding these, playing to them or manipulating them you can, in theory, persuade anyone to do anything. What is more interesting, perhaps, to us is if we inadvertently cross or contradict one of these deeply embedded drives, things can go horribly wrong very quickly. Of course we must remember that it takes two to tango and our own drives can get in the way too. Would we sacrifice our pride and status simply to change another's point of view, or more prosaically is it better to prove the customer wrong than to sell them something? To complicate matters a bit more, although we all have these drives, different people with different personalities have differing proportions of them. The skilful persuader can recognize the predominant drive and work on it to achieve the best result. The eight drives, as I see them, are:

1. Biological needs – hunger, thirst, warmth, and so on.

2. Sex.

3. Dependency – help, protection, and guidance from authority.

4. Dominance – being accepted by others as the leader. Being allowed to do all the talking and make the decisions.

5. Affiliation – a feeling of belonging, warmth and friendship from our associates.

6. Aggression – domination through physical and verbal intimidation.

7. Self-esteem – this is the desire we have for other people to confirm and support our ego ideal.

8. Motivation – this drive moves us forward to achieve our desires, wealth, status, and acknowledgment (even fame).

Biological Needs

This can be a difficult one to play on. You could lock your subject in a room without food or water until they agree to change their mind. This could be called torture – the subject can get a bit surly and resentful and, to be fair, the penal system has never had much luck with it.

Sex

I don't think this is the sort of book that needs to go there!

Dependency

We get that installed into us at a very early age; let go of Mummy's hand against orders and when we fall flat on our face we get, "There you go, little breeches, if you'd held on to Mummy's hand that would never have happened." That happens to all of us but some get the, "If only you had listened to me" stuff for most of our lives. It conditions us to depend on those we respect and trust, and never forgive those who betray us. To that subject we need to appear trustworthy, be trustworthy, and offer safety in the shape of get-outs. Honesty is the best policy with this subject. They can be very indecisive so sometimes you need to make their decision for them, but woe betide you if you are dishonest.

"Oh, I'm not sure; I can't make up my mind."

"Do you mind if I make a suggestion?" Wait for the answer as long as it takes. "I think that the best one for you is this one."

"Are you sure?"

"I am, but if after a few days you are not happy, bring it back and you can try the other one."

Affiliation

We all love to belong to something. It all starts in the playground – there is nothing lonelier than the new kid, alone in the corner, with no one to play with. Even if you want to be a Hell's Angel, you have to prove your worth as a prospect for years before they will accept you. In some of the primitive tribes, being excluded from the group as a punishment can actually kill the subject. The skilful persuader can recognize this need to belong, and makes statements like, "I know it's a lot of money to invest, but intelligent investors like yourself are rushing to buy this". Not only does this statement acknowledge that they are an 'intelligent investor' but it makes them feel as though they belong to a group. If you need any evidence of this, watch any beer advert with groups of cheery knowing men, or any cosmetic adverts which almost inevitably play the tune, 'Here Comes the Girls!' We all love to belong and knowing and using this is a very powerful tool in our persuasion box of tricks.

Dominance

This is a very topsy-turvy, back to front drive. People who have the desire to be accepted as the leader rarely have great leadership qualities. They sometimes bully their partner if they are lucky enough to have one, but often slip up and are in fact bullied themselves, so they are ready to take it out on anyone they meet. Sometimes they are the spoilt sons and daughters who have inherited the family business, maybe they are the petty bureaucrat, but in any event they would dogmatically expect deference where deference isn't deserved. For us the reward for having to deal with these ghastly people is that they are easy to manipulate simply by managing their huge egos – dodgy lines like, "I respect your opinion", "You are an intelligent person", "I wonder if you could give me some advice based on your enormous experience". Sometimes I will see how far I can push it before they rumble me – they never do, but be warned, try this with the wrong person and you will be toast. So keep your wits about you and make sure you 'qualify' your subject which brings us neatly to:

Aggression

There are aggressive people and there are people who sometimes act aggressively. What made them aggressive? Was it you? Or was it that their car broke down, the town is seething with shoppers, or their relationship is on the rocks, or maybe they've just lost their job. They fly at you with, "Hey, you! Don't just stand there, explain this." This is where we need to understand behaviour. As we interact, we affect each other's behaviour. That person's aggression will, in the normal world, cause us to react – either with aggression ourselves if we think we're hard enough, or fear if we aren't (audience with me all the way but I shook them off at the airport). But now we are professional persuaders, aren't we? What persuasion is about is to change the other person's emotional position. We need to indulge in behaviour modification. We can adopt a set of behaviours that alter the way the other person behaves. First of all, take them seriously.

"Good morning. What can I do for you?"

"Don't good morning me, you little worm!"

Do not react, but sympathise with their distress.

"I am sorry that you are upset. Let me try and help."

"You can't help; it was your company who got me in this mess. I'm going to sue."

Do not say, "I'm sure there is no need for that" or "I'm sure it's not that bad", or "That's nothing to get upset about", because they ARE upset. However outrageous, unfair, or even petty their demands or grievance, treat it like the most important issue in the world. Ask questions and listen; not just any old listening, either, but sincere Active Listening where you nod, give eye contact, write notes, and give prompts like, "Go on", "Really, I am so sorry to hear that", "Yes, yes, I see", "So tell me, how did this..."

Your Behaviour will Change Their behaviour

If we act with warmth and sincerity, our choice of these behaviours will alter the other person's behaviour. This is persuasion at its best. No, the aggressive maniac won't lie down with the lamb but you stand a much better chance.

This is one of the most powerful techniques I know if you want to 'Win Friends and Influence People' (to pinch a book title). Just think of every interaction you ever have with another person. From burger-flipper to brain surgeon, they all leave you with feelings that I could ask you about after the event.

"How is your burger? How do you feel about the kid that served you?"

"What kid?"

This is about our:

Self Esteem

To use the posh name, this is the Ego Ideal. The kid in the burger bar had no effect on us at all. That miserable, difficult, bureaucrat in the government office can actually make us feel bad. We can choose to make our interaction positive. Just try it, not for persuasive reasons to start with but to form a habit of making people feel good whenever they are around you.

"What a lovely shop."

"Your kid seems extremely bright."

One little warning, don't pick things that aren't true or you will be rumbled.

The effect of doing this is stunning. People smile back when you smile. They light up when you notice and appreciate their efforts but, most of all, they seek you out and become your fans.

Motivation

People have a need to achieve in order to acquire status and by the same token to acquire positions that reflect their status. This drive should be more of a warning to the aspiring persuader not to let their own standards slip. There is a ghastly expression that says, "If you want to soar with the eagles, don't hang around with the turkeys." Of course everyone thinks they are an eagle so make sure you don't look like a turkey – cheap clothes, chipped cups, poor notepaper, bad timekeeping, these all scream turkey. If your subject sinks into your luxurious soft leather, while sipping espresso from your Spode china, they may (a) feel treated like an eagle, and (b) see you as a fellow-soarer. Run-down businesses smell of defeat so be professional at every step.

The Body Says It All

We now get into the tricky area of non-verbal communication. There are those who would have you believe that a huge percentage of our communication is non-verbal – closed or open postures, handshakes, chin-rubbing and gaze. This may or may not be true, but if you watch a film in a language you do not understand, you will not know what it is about. The man who shook his fist at the man who subsequently shot him, you could fairly judge that they may not have been getting on too well, but what was it all about? No idea!

What the other person's non-verbal activities do, however, is to give us clues, clues that we should not ignore. The fiddling, fidgeting, and leaning away from us may suggest boredom or disengagement. Covering the mouth and eye rubbing can suggest dishonesty. These basic clues should prompt subtle questioning to test our position.

"Do you have the paperwork to support that?"

"May I ask you something?"

Pauses, timing, questions, will put us back in control, but what is more fascinating is whether body language can tell us the other person's thought processes. Perhaps if we control the body we can generate the thoughts. One of the key areas of non-verbal communication is the human face, and eye contact is vital. Good eye contact combined with an open body posture are all good signs. So try this. If your subject has their arms folded and they are looking down and kicking the dust, offer them your folder, document, or whatever – they have to unfold or hold it. Don't let go, so now they are holding one bit and you are holding the other. Point to the subject with your pen and then lift it from the page. The pen lifts their eye-line to yours where you can make your point "most sincerely"!

Control Yourself!

The final point is that we need to control our own non-verbal signals: open palms, good eye contact. Get hold of a good book on body language and, rather than use it to spot the subject's intentions which is tedious and distracting, look up all the bad signs like hand rubbing, mouth covering, and general shiftiness, and stop doing any of them yourself. One small wrinkle – if you are not sure of your case and you find it difficult to give eye contact, look at the subject's forehead. Apparently this will make you look very sincere.

Perhaps one day I will write a whole book on the subject of the psychology of persuasion, but for now this concise section should give you enough insight to supplement your meticulous planning and immaculate presentation to ensure a successful outcome to each of your well considered persuasion journeys.

POINTS TO PONDER ON CHAPTER 20

1. Every decision we make and everything we believe happens inside our head. If you can change someone's thought processes, you can change everything they believe to be true.

2. The choice of words can be very powerful. There is a big difference between 'honest city worker' and 'fat cat banker'.

3. Tell stories that paint pictures to avoid boredom. Even the truth is no use if it isn't fun to listen to.

4. Proving that someone is wrong is just about the worst thing you can do. Remember to preserve their pride.

5. We need someone we can depend on to be respected, to belong, and to believe in ourselves, as much as we need air, water, and food.

6. Even if we are met with aggression, we can choose behaviours that change their behaviour.

7. Appearance is everything. If you look like a turkey you will get stuffed like a turkey.

GOODBYE FOR NOW

I meet so many eager, talented people who somehow just fail to reach their potential or to achieve their dreams. Then, on the other hand, I meet others who seem to have far more wealth, success or fame than they deserve. I know you are full of good things, you have talents that you would love a chance to use, ideas that you feel would benefit all those who took them up, but somehow luck doesn't seem to come your way. Well guess what? Luck doesn't come into it. When you see those vacuous celebs who are just rich and famous simply for being famous, the Press describe them as, "self promoting". That is the key. That is what they do. They promote themselves. They don't wait like us mortals to be promoted, they 'persuade' others of their value. However shallow these celebrities may seem, they have their journey clearly planned. They intend to succeed. No conversation or discussion is wasted, no opportunity is lost, and when there is a queue they are at the front of it.

Persuasion is about intent. When you are persuasive you have conversations with an intended outcome. You will use strategy and plan an outcome that you want. It is a very rare thing to do and if you can master the skills required you will get those lost chances you feel you deserve. The only time we seem to do it naturally is when we are looking for romance. We see someone we fancy, we talk about the weather, the band, our home town, and about their interests – and we laugh at their jokes. Then, if we feel we are making progress, we discuss an opportunity for another meeting. All of this flim flam is to hide our true objective – you know what that is and the rest is window dressing as we work towards our goal with intent. So is it the one who leads the way, makes the running, and tells the story, the one who wins? No, not always. They say a man chases a woman until she catches him, not with the gift of the gab but with the gift of the earhole. The winner is the one with the desire, the intent, and the power to persuade.

I would so love you to benefit from reading this book, it would delight and thrill me even if all it did was give you the opportunities that you deserve but have missed simply because you have failed to persuade.

With that nugget, I feel that it is about time for me to ride off into the sunset. Just let me leave you with these thoughts:

♩ If you can persuade anybody to do anything, there is nothing in life you cannot have.

♩ Just make sure you are in control of the whole process.

♩ If you can see it as a journey, that can be most helpful.

♩ Be clear of your destination.

♩ Understand the obstacles you will encounter.

♩ Do not underestimate the distance.

♩ Recognize landmarks along the way.

♩ Have a clear honest map that includes a beginning and an end.

♩ Make sure you are properly equipped for every eventuality.

BON VOYAGE!

SOME INTERESTING READING

John Fenton, *How to Sell Against Competition*, Pan Books, 1986.

Heinz M Goldman, *How to Win Customers*, Staples Press, 1958.

Dale Carnegie, *How to Win Friends and Influence People*, Vermilion, 2006.

Eric Berne, *Games People Play*, Penguin, 2010.

Michael Argyle, *The Psychology of Interpersonal Behaviour*, Penguin Books, 1994.

Niccolo Machiavelli, *The Prince*, Longman, 2004.
Great for mind-games.

Roger Fisher, William Ury and Bruce Patton, *Getting to Yes*, Random House Business Books, 2003.
Great book on negotiating.

Ricardo Semler, *The Seven Day Weekend*, Century, 2004.
Great book.

My previous books on persuasion:

The Writing on the Wall: The Campaign for Commonsense Business, Capstone, 2002.

Resistance is Useless: The Art of Business Persuasion, Capstone, 2003.

Go It Alone: The Streetwise Secrets of Self-employment, Capstone, 2003.

The Way of the Dog: The Art of Making Success Inevitable, Capstone, 2005.